Y0-BCP-252

PIAGET—A PRACTICAL CONSIDERATION

PIAGET—A PRACTICAL CONSIDERATION

A consideration of the general theories and work of Jean Piaget, with an account of a short follow up study of his work on the development of the concept of geometry

BY

G. A. HELMORE

Diploma in Primary Education
University of Leeds Institute of Education
Headmaster of Parc Eglos C.P. School, Helston, Cornwall

PERGAMON PRESS

Oxford · London · Edinburgh · New York
Toronto · Sydney · Paris · Braunschweig

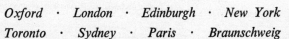

Pergamon Press Ltd., Headington Hill Hall, Oxford
4 & 5 Fitzroy Square, London W.1
Pergamon Press (Scotland) Ltd., 2 & 3 Teviot Place, Edinburgh 1
Pergamon Press Inc., Maxwell House, Fairview Park, Elmsford,
New York 10523
Pergamon of Canada Ltd., 207 Queen's Quay West, Toronto 1
Pergamon Press (Aust.) Pty. Ltd., 19a Boundary Street,
Rushcutters Bay, N.S.W. 2011, Australia
Pergamon Press S.A.R.L., 24 rue des Écoles, Paris 5ᵉ
Vieweg & Sohn GmbH, Burgplatz 1, Braunschweig

Library of Congress Catalog Card No. 75–94933

Printed in Great Britain by A. Wheaton & Co., Exeter

08 006892 8 (flexicover)
08 006893 6 (hard cover)

CONTENTS

INTRODUCTION

This short book is a brief statement of the theory of Jean Piaget concerning the general pattern of intellectual development in children which he claims to have found. It also includes an account, and consideration of the results, of a follow-up study conducted among children drawn from two English primary schools in differing environments. The book has been deliberately kept short, for teachers and student-teachers do not have time to spare reading unnecessarily wordy expositions; and since they also do not have time to look up continuous cross-references these have been kept to an absolute minimum too. However, for those readers who wish to read further on the subject of Piaget's work, Appendix 2 may prove useful.

Appendix 1 has been included for several reasons, most of which are obvious. One that should be emphasized is that any reader of this book can conduct one of Piaget's experiments himself. For every teacher it will be a revelation. I have heard it described by a colleague as "Taking the top off the child's head and watching the wheels go round". Try it and see.

I should like to conclude this short introduction by thanking Dr. K. Lovell, of the University of Leeds Institute of Education, for all his help. It was as a result of his lectures that I first began to understand and appreciate Piaget's work, and I believe he has summed the matter up in his statement in those lectures that "When Piaget's true worth is known he will be owed as much by teachers, as Freud is by psychologists". The protocols used in the conduct of the experiments, and printed in Appendix 1, were drawn up by Dr. Lovell, and I am most grateful for his permission to reprint them in this book.

CHAPTER 1

JEAN PIAGET AND HIS APPROACH TO HIS WORK

JEAN PIAGET is the son of a Swiss historian. He was born at Neuchatel in 1896. At the age of 7 he wrote a little book in pencil entitled *Our Birds*, and so his first love, zoology, was declared to the world. When he was a 10-year-old boy, Piaget systematically watched and noted the behaviour of an albino sparrow, and his written observations were printed in the local journal of natural history. The curator of the Neuchatel museum, a leading authority on molluscs, then encouraged his natural interest, and directed it to the task of classifying and labelling the specimens of freshwater shells to be found in the nearby lake, and also to investigating the different types of snail and mussel to be found there. The results of this piece of study were printed in a series of articles in the *Revue Suisse de Zoologie* while he was still at school. In 1918, having graduated in Natural Sciences, Piaget obtained a doctorate with a thesis entitled "Alpine Molluscs".

As a result of family upbringing and his education, Jean Piaget now found himself in the centre of a conflict of ideas. His was a strictly religious family, and he realized increasingly that the biologist's view of human nature that he held, as a result of his education, appeared to be opposed to the doctrines held by his religion. He sought refuge from the emotional crisis that resulted by writing a philosophical novel which dealt with the problem of the two irreconcilable viewpoints, the hero's solution was, to quote Burt,[2] "to investigate how human knowledge has evolved, and to do so by applying the methods, not of the philosopher, but of the biologist himself". He seems to have been following his hero's example ever since.

1

Piaget now enrolled in the psychological laboratory at Zurich. There he attended Jung's lectures and amongst others read the works of Herbert Spencer which exercised considerable influence on his later writings. In 1919 he went to Paris where Dr. Simon (Binet's collaborator on the scale of intelligence tests that bear his name) set him the task of standardizing Burt's reasoning tests for Parisian children. He commenced this task without much enthusiasm and soon decided that it was far more important to discover how each child reached his conclusions, especially when those conclusions were wrong, than it was to establish norms.

On his return to Switzerland, 2 years later, he was invited to become Director of Studies at the Rousseau Institute of Geneva, which is now part of the University of Geneva, and is known as the Institute of Educational Science. At the age of 26 he accepted the appointment, and has remained there working with research students ever since, studying the mental development of the child. (His present appointment is that of Professor of Psychology at Geneva, and until recently he was also Professor at the Sorbonne.) In his work the problem of Piaget has always been the same, and it arises out of Spencer's own doctrine of adaptation. How does the growing child adjust himself to the world in which he lives? How are we to account for the constant recurrence of what, to the rational adult, seem extreme instances of maladjustment?

Jean Piaget's search for answers to these questions was begun in the familiar form of keeping careful records of what young children said and did. He very soon found these methods insufficient and unsatisfactory, however, and he started to develop the ingenious techniques for which he is now world famous. The results of his work have been steadily published to the world in a flow of books and other publications which has gone on since 1924. Much of his technique of investigation seems to be the very antithesis of normal methods of scientific investigation for he gives his imagination a free hand. He is trying all the time to get inside the mind of the child in order that he may see the world from the child's own standpoint. A much-quoted example of this was the set of experiments which involved his joining in each child's favourite game on an equal footing with the child, which included such activities as learning how to make a good shot at marbles, how to make a bad shot, and even how to cheat![(9)]

Piaget's published works are extremely difficult to read, expecially in the theoretical sections. There are several reasons for this and the first, of course, is that he is investigating and writing about an extremely intricate and involved process. Another minor cause is that all of his publications are written in French and it is often extremely difficult to find exact English equivalents for the original French terms used; however, by far the greatest share of the difficulty arises from the fact that, as has already been described, Piaget's own intellectual development and education has been so very comprehensive and complex. The following quotation from Barbel Inhelder, one of Piaget's collaborators, amplifies this point;

> The conception of mental development as it appears in the works of M. Piaget is somewhat disconcerting, not because of the facts, but because of the terminology. M. Piaget, who is a zoologist by training, an epistem-ologist by vocation and a logician by method, employs a terminology as yet not much used in Psychology. He expresses himself mainly in terms of structures, which by definition are systems of mental operations obeying definite laws of composition, such as, for example, the mathe-matical laws of group and lattice. According to a number of cyberneti-cists, structures are as much physiological as mental. It seems necessary to keep in mind this triple orientation—biological, epistemological and logico-mathematical—which is continually reflected in Piaget's vocabu-lary, in order to find one's way easily among the Geneva studies. But once these characteristics are appreciated the data and laws deriving from them become clear and easily verified.[(14)]

Despite what appears to be a somewhat over-optimistic claim in the final sentence of this quotation, a careful consideration of the whole quotation does clearly illumine the problem. Piaget's terminology, to those who have not studied his sciences, makes the reading of his books exceptionally difficult, for he so seldom defines the terms he uses, and they often appear to the non-scientist reader most obscure. However, with familiarity comes comprehension, partly from context and partly by a slow growth of understanding (or so I believe to be the case), for after the first three or four of Piaget's books, carefully read, the terminology becomes commonplace, accepted, and even generally understood, but still remains very difficult to explain to others without using almost equally difficult terms.

CHAPTER 2

A SUMMARY OF THE GENERAL THEORIES OF PIAGET— THE PIAGETIAN CONCEPT OF INTELLIGENCE AND ITS DEVELOPMENT

PIAGET'S approach is a genetic and biological one. "He attempts to distinguish stages of development in the evolution of thought, and to show how each stage reveals a progressive sequence from simpler to more complex levels of organisation".[12] To do this he has had to develop his own methods which are described later—the Piagetian experiments. These latter require a child to solve a problem, and the basic plan of each experiment is such as to reveal the stages of development toward the full pattern of thought processes involved in the final solution of the problem. Each child's answers, therefore, when recorded, enable the experimenter to place him at his stage of development in the evolution of that particular pattern of thought.

Chronologically, Piaget was at first a biologist, and so one can understand his selected starting point for all of his theories on the development of intelligence—it is that higher psychological functions grow out of biological mechanisms. One can also understand that it is logical for him to describe the actions producing this development in biological terms, and so to develop his doctrine of *maturation.*

Piaget[10] defines intelligence as "the state of *equilibrium* towards which tend all successive adaptations of a sensori-motor and cognitive nature, as well as all *assimilatory* and *accommodatory* interactions between the organism and the environment". He

5

looks upon the growth of intelligence as the growth of the ability to achieve equilibrium at an increasingly high level of complexity. The meaning of the term "equilibrium" becomes clearer from a consideration of a further statement: "Intelligence is adaptation ... adaptation must be described as an equilibrium between the action of the organism on the environment and vice versa." By "the action of the organism upon the environment", Piaget means *assimilation*, in so far as this action depends on previous behaviour involving the same or similar objects (or circumstances). "Physiologically" Piaget[10] states:

> "the organism absorbs substances and changes them into something compatible with its own substance. Now, psychologically, the same is true except that the modifications with which it is then concerned are no longer of a physico-chemical order but entirely functional, and are determined by movement, perception or the interplay of real or potential actions (conceptual operations, etc.). Mental assimilation is thus the incorporation of objects into patterns of behaviour, these patterns being none other than the whole gamut of actions capable of active repetition.

By *assimilation*, then, it seems that Piaget means the way in which the mind takes its continuing experience of objects, circumstances, situations, etc., and orders them into schemata of thought for future use.

The action of the environment on the organism he terms *accommodation*. In the physiological sense "the individual never suffers the impact of surrounding stimuli as such, but they simply modify the assimilatory cycle". Piaget[10] states that the equivalent is true in the psychological sense: "the pressure of circumstances always leads, not to a passive submission to them, but to a simple modification of the action affecting them."

By *accommodation*, then, it seems that Piaget means the way in which the mind modifies its schemata in the light of new experience.

In his studies of the progress made by children towards higher levels of equilibrium, there are two key factors emphasized in Piaget's work. The first of these is the extent to which an organism can control shifts of orientation; the second is the ability of the organism to develop *operations*. An operation is an action that has been internalized into a thought process. The act of thinking involves the use of groups or systems of such operations. Piaget[10] lists five properties of such groups or systems of operations:

(i) *Composition.* Any two units can be combined to produce a new unit.

(ii) *Reversibility.* Two units combined may be separated again.

(iii) *Associativity.* The same results may be obtained by combining units in different ways.

(iv) *Identity.* Combining an element with its inverse annuls it.

(v) (a) *Tautology.* A classification or relation which is repeated is not changed.

(b) *Iteration.* A number combined with itself gives a new number.

Operations and their groupings (i.e. thought processes and their groupings) are the main object of Piaget's developmental approach to concept formation. From his many experiments performed by children of all ages he claims that there are five main stages in the development of a concept, through which the vast majority of children pass, it being remembered that the bright child will pass through the stages more quickly and the dull child may fail to reach the final stage(s) of maturity. The final statement suggested by Piaget's work, then, is that what we term "thinking", for example the ability to solve theoretical and practical problems—the ability to make reasoned judgements, the recognition of relationships, and the associations of ideas, etc. —is, in fact, only the result of a system of thinking that has been slowly built up within the brain. Our ideas of number, space, time, weight, measurement, etc., are not innate, but are built up piecemeal as we live our early lives, firstly through the sensory and motor activities of our early infancy and then at an accelerated rate through our association with the people around us and our developing ability to understand and use language. These background schemata so built, then, are the foundations for all our subsequent thinking, will always affect it, and without them, suggests Piaget, "thinking" would be virtually impossible.

The Piagetian Stages of Development

(i) THE SENSORI-MOTOR STAGE (0–2 YEARS)

"In this phase the infant can perform only motor actions—manipulating objects in trial and error fashion."[12] At birth the baby has innate reflexes only. For some weeks his world consists of visual patterns, etc., which follow in a temporal sequence that is so temporal that the child does not have a chance to arrive at any real understanding of the situation. He co-ordinates perception and movement but without any real awareness of the situation. Objects are without permanence at first, but gradually, because of his actions, the baby builds up a picture of the world as a succession of objects with permanence in its surroundings. During the early months of life the distinction between self and non-self is not realized, but he finally regards himself as one object amongst many. The child starts to learn through interaction between himself and his environment, his actions of assimilation and accommodation commence; he learns, for example, that certain movements in certain directions carried out at certain times lead to certain results.

By about the first birthday the ability to imitate makes its appearance and the child tends to assimilate the movement repertoire of others. During the second year this developing ability to imitate is extended to "deferred imitation"—the imitation of an absent person. Imagery is deferred imitation and so the first indications of imagery are seen in the second year of life and with imagery comes symbolic or make-believe play. Language develops too, and the child learns to use words as symbols. By the time he is 2 the child can invent new patterns of behaviour by means of words, actions, and symbolic play, and shows he can understand the results of his actions before he performs them. True thought is thus commencing for he is internalizing some of his actions into thought, "but it goes without saying that this organization, circumscribed as it is by the limitations of action, still does not constitute a form of thought".[10]

(ii) THE PRECONCEPTUAL STAGE (2–4 years)

"After the appearance of language or, more precisely, the symbolic function that makes its acquisition possible ($1\frac{1}{2}$–2 years), there begins a period which lasts until nearly 4 years and sees the development of a symbolic and preconceptual thought".[10] The deferred imitation and imagery development commenced in the previous stage develops still further and with it the rapid development of the understanding of symbols follows. "Preconcepts are the notions which the child attaches to the first verbal signs he learns to use."[10] These preconcepts lie somewhere between a concept of an individual object and a concept of the general class of the object. To the child at this stage "dog" and "dogs" are indistinguishable, "he cannot yet cope with general classes, being unable to distinguish between 'all' and 'some'."[10]

Furthermore, the child is unable to argue in a deductive manner from the general to the particular or vice versa—inductively. Piaget states that he argues "transductively"—from the particular to the particular, "it merely consists of a sequence of actions symbolized in thought, a true 'mental experiment'."[10] If two objects or situations are alike in some respects, then arguing transductively the child will claim that they are alike in all respects.

Symbols and the objects which they represent are frequently confused and the child has an egocentric attitude to his world.

(iii) THE INTUITIVE STAGE (4–7 years)

"From 4 to about 7 or 8 years, there is developed, as a closely linked continuation of the previous stage, an intuitive thought whose progressive articulations lead to the threshold of the operation." It is in this stage that Piaget states it is possible to give the child short experiments, "in which he has to manipulate experimental objects [which] enable us to obtain regular answers and to converse with him. This fact alone indicates a new structure".[10]

Intuitive thought, in the Piagetian meaning, is thought determined by a way of looking, by perception. During this period there is a very considerable increase in the internalization of thought, but the child can only consider one action or one variable at a time. Reversibility is not achieved, although there is an advance towards its achievement. This means the child is still unable in thought to return to his starting point. For example if the shape of a lump of plasticine is altered, he believes that the amount of the plasticine in the lump alters too. The permanent nature of the quantity irrespective of shape is beyond him, his thought is affected only by his perception of the alteration of one dimension, e.g. it has been flattened, therefore there is less—what Piaget calls "conservation" is not realized. To repeat—the child is only able to consider one "view" of the situation, but as he progresses through this stage he shows a developing ability to attain different "views" and when he learns to co-ordinate these he will achieve "conservation" and this stage is behind him. This stage can be observed in many of Piaget's experiments, in which the child will commence his answering from the level of internalized thought, but as the experiment progresses and the gap between the reasoned answer and the perceptive observation widens, the former will eventually be abandoned and all subsequent answers will be given at a perceptive level only.

(iv) CONCRETE OPERATIONS (7–11 YEARS)

"From 7–8 to 11–12 years 'concrete operations' are organized, i.e. operational groupings of thought concerning objects that can be manipulated or known through the senses."[10]

In this stage reversibility is developed and thus logical thought begins to develop. Logical thought arises when the child has built up a stock of concrete concepts which he begins to manipulate into a system. This stage is of operational thought development and in it the child develops three kinds of concepts. The first of these is the concept of classification, the inclusion of one class within another—for example the child can group together all bricks of a similar colour from a collection of bricks of mixed colours. The second concept is that of seriation, of ordering in size in a systematic way. From such an activity and understanding the child arrives at a conception of relationships between objects. The third concept is that of number and it arises out of the first two. The number system is the product of the joint concepts of class and relationship, e.g. the number 7 involves the ability to see seven similar objects and then to see their relationship to the numbers 6 and 8.

Despite the conceptual development that is taking place, however, the child is still limited in the number of variables he can consider and still achieve conservation—a third variable will still defeat him.[12] The ability to deal with more than two variables is achieved at the end of this stage and the five properties of systems of operations (composition, reversibility, associativity, identity, tautology, and iteration) have taken their place in the child's thought process.

(v) FORMAL OPERATIONS (11 YEARS ONWARDS)

"Finally, from 11 to 12 years and during adolescence, formal thought is perfected and its groupings characterize the completion of reflective intelligence."[10] The child is no longer deterred by his perception, nor limited to the concrete situation, he can consider a number of variables in turn.[11] He can increasingly set up anticipatory schema in his mind, he can manipulate in his mind the propositions that link the classes and relationships, he can set up an hypothesis. There have, in fact, developed four abilities:

(a) The ability to reason on relations between propositions.
(b) The ability to consider and use all possible disjunctions and combinations.

   (c) The ability to use both inversion and the reciprocal in a single system.
   (d) The ability to increase understanding of action and reaction.

The experiments used by Piaget and Inhelder[11] demonstrate that these four abilities are clearly developing in the adolescent, and ability (b) will enable him to think and reason inductively, generalizing from a number of instances. The child has reached "the structure of the final equilibrium to which concrete operations tend, when they are reflected in more general systems linking together the propositions that express them."[10]

CHAPTER 3

THE PIAGETIAN EXPERIMENTS

THE published works of Jean Piaget fall into two main periods. The first of these extended from 1924 to 1932. During this time seven major works were published, of which we may concern ourselves with five (English translation titles), namely:

1924, *Judgment and Reasoning in the Child.*
1924, *The Language and Thought of the Child.*
1926, *The Child's Conception of the World.*
1927, *The Child's Conception of Physical Causality.*
1932, *The Moral Judgment of the Child.*

These books published the results of Piaget's studies of the development of the thought, language, and moral judgement of the child and were his early exposition of how a child's thought progressed from the illogical to the logical, and from the precausal to the causal. Piaget explains this development by stating that the child has to overcome his initial egocentrism of thought and has to differentiate and reintegrate his own viewpoint in relation to the world about him.

The main criticisms of these early works, as recorded by Nathan Isaacs were, "that there was much to object to, and even to reject, in the way in which most of his material seemed to have been gathered," and that "his actual findings were more open to doubt, whilst . . . his 'working hypothesis' went very much further than in more recent years".[3]

The second period of Piaget's work commenced in 1936. (The opinion has been expressed by Aebli[1] that this period ended in 1948 and that a third "philosophic" period has now commenced with the publication of his last two major works.) During this period the following have been his most important publications translated into English:

1936, *The Origins of Intelligence in Children.*
1937, *The Child's Construction of Reality.*
1941, *The Child's Conception of Number.*
1945, *Play, Dreams and Imitation in Childhood.*
1947, *The Psychology of Intelligence.*
1948, *The Child's Conception of Space.*
1948, *The Child's Conception of Geometry,*
1955, *The Growth of Logical Thinking from Childhood to Adolescence.*

A study of the growth of certain concepts, together with the formulation of a theory that intellectual growth follows a universal pattern of development through certain well-defined stages, as maturation proceeds, has been the main work of this period. These works have aroused less criticism than those of the earlier period because: "for mere verbal questionings he [Piaget] substituted concrete experimental situations, very much like games, in which the child was invited to join. . . . And the interpretation did not go beyond the actual facts."[3] In the books of this period Piaget has occasionally had the assistance of collaborators and he has adopted a recognizable pattern of approach.

This pattern of approach is the use of the now famous "Piagetian experiment". To investigate some point of inquiry a sample of children is taken and each child in the sample is required to take part in one or more experiments. In these "experiments" he is faced with a series of problems, in the solving of which, by means of careful questioning, the investigator can persuade the child to externalize his thought. From the pattern of the responses given by the children, of different chronological ages and levels of mental development, the developmental stages of the growth of the concept are made available for our study.

For the results of the experiments so conducted to be valid

certain factors are important. The first of these is that the sample of children undergoing the experiments should be a satisfactory one. This demands that it should include a full range of intelligence in each age group and also children from the widest possible variety of backgrounds. (In passing it is interesting to note that it would seem from Piaget's books that his own samples of children used in his experiments are sometimes fairly small.) The second important factor is that the children should demonstrate in their experiments their optimum performance levels, to enable valid comparisons to be made. In order that this may occur it is vital that the experimenter shall establish a good rapport with the children in the sample. It is quite obvious from the conversations between Piaget and "his children", reported verbatim in his books, that Piaget has achieved such a rapport.

For the teacher in the classroom who wishes to carry out some of the Piagetian experiments the following advice is offered. A reasonable, small-size sample may be gained by taking five children from each primary school chronological age group if the school is streamed—one top A, one middle A streamer, one top B, one middle B streamer, and one top C streamer. This will give a slightly favoured picture due to the omission of the bottom C streamer, but since many of these latter have not progressed beyond the first stage of development, they frequently add little to our knowledge of the developmental stages we wish to discover and examine. (Where a school is unstreamed the equivalents to the selections suggested above may be taken on the results of a non-verbal and verbal intelligence test for the age group.) In order that good rapport may be established between the experimenter and the children it is suggested that the experimenter should first meet them in small groups, possibly during a classroom activity period; a second meeting should then follow, after a day or so, when the experimenter should meet each child singly and engage him (her) in everyday conversation, various simple details being recorded such as date of birth, notes of special interests, and details of family background. These latter are most useful for they may be used at the third (and subsequent) meetings to place the child at ease before introducing him (her) to the first two or three experiments, which are best referred to as "puzzles" when talking to the children. Two experiments, or three at the most, may be given at each meeting with each child, to avoid loss of interest or overtiring, resulting in a decline in performance level, and the necessary steps need to be taken to avoid a transfer of information from one child to another before the latter has been set the puzzles.

The procedure outlined above was adopted by the author in carrying out the experiments described and recorded in the following chapter. The sample was, in fact, chosen with great care from two schools showing widely differing environments, and was based upon the class teachers' assessments as well as the results of intelligence tests, and great care was taken to see that the subject was still interested when tackling the puzzle, that tension was kept out of the experiment room, and that no attempt was made to hurry the child in his attempts to solve the problem. However, a study of the table of results facing p. 32 will show that in the first-year junior chronological group 4 A-stream children were chosen. These children were all in a class in which the experimenter spent a considerable time each week, and this was done so that their performance in the unstructured situations arising in the classroom could be compared with those in the experiments. They were good A children, but not exceptionally so.

CHAPTER 4

SIX SELECTED PIAGETIAN EXPERIMENTS

THE six experiments described below are adapted from the book *The Child's Conception of Geometry* (Routledge, 1960). This book is the second half of a two-volume study of which *The Child's Conception of Space* (Routledge, 1956) is the other half. The aim of the book is to give an account of Piaget's investigation of the problems of measurement and metrical geometry, and by means of this investigation to show the stages of development through which the child's concept progresses.

Piaget states that "Measurement is a synthesis of sub-division and change of position", and he investigates these two factors separately. The account of his experiments shows a progression of development through three or four stages from a complete faith in visual perception, through the evolution of hand and arm movements as an intermediate measure, to the use of a common measure which could finally be applied by the operation of unit iteration. The final stage of development of the concept he terms "Conservation", by which he means that length (or area or volume, etc.) is unaltered by change of position, or change in the order of the elements composing the whole.

The descriptions which follow are, in certain cases, slightly modified forms of the experiments used by Piaget. These modifications do not, it is felt, render them in any way invalid for comparing their results with English children, with those of Piaget with Swiss children. The main difference lies in a more frequent use of questions such as "Why?" by the experimenter, in order that there should be a minimum of doubt as to what stage of development the child has reached.

17

Experiment 1. The Length of Lines and the Coincidence of their Extremities

The child is presented with a short stick of wood and a longer undulating thread of plasticine. The ends of the plasticine are made to coincide exactly with those of the stick, which is placed beside it, a few millimetres from it (Fig. 1). The child is now asked to compare the lengths of the two objects. The question used is, "Are they the same length, or is one longer than the other?" Following his reply the supplementary question "Why?" is put. If the subject says they are equal, he is made to run his fingers along the two lines and the question is then repeated. If he persists

Fig. 1.

in saying they are the same the question is put, "If there were two ants or two little men, and they walked along those lines, which would they find the longer?" Finally the child is shown what happens when the "snake" of plasticine is straightened out. When he readily admits that the "snake" is now longer than the stick, the snake is twisted back into its original shape with end points coinciding with those of the stick and the original question is repeated.

The stages of development described by Piaget are as follows:

Stage 1:   The length of a line is estimated solely in terms

of its end points without reference to its recti-
linearity or lack of it. (Sample age up to 5:3.)

Sub-stage IIA: Responses intermediate between stage I and
sub-stage IIB. Replies are inconsistent, some
correct, some incorrect.

Sub-stage IIB: Intuitive composition of distance is commencing;
length is realized as not a matter of simple
consideration of the end points. (Sample age
4:10 onwards.)

Stage III: Was not attainable in this experiment due to its
simplicity.

Experiment 2. Subdividing a Straight Line

This experiment, as described by Piaget, is very long. As it was
felt that the essence of the experiment was contained in a selection
from the many situations described in the book, four were selected
and used.

Two straight lines, A_1C_1 and A_2C_2 (or A_3C_3 if the second line
is longer than the first) are represented by lengths of string or
wire attached to nails on strips of wood. A bead is threaded on
each wire and placed at A_1 and A_2 (or A_3) (Fig. 2). In the following
separate situations the child is asked the following questions.

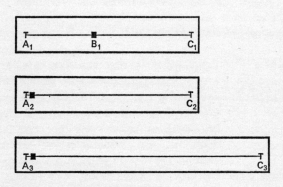

Fig. 2.

"The bead is a train travelling along a railway line. My train is going this far [moves his bead from A_1 to B_1]. I want your train to do a journey that is just as long as mine; one the same length. Start your bead from here [A_2]". Pause. "Where will you go?" "How can you be sure?"

Situation 1a. The two strings A_1C_1 and A_2C_2 are parallel and identical in length (30 in.). The various points on both lines are in direct alignment, so that to find B_2 the subject has only to show a point on A_2C_2 immediately facing B_1. (Distance A_1B_1 approximately 6 in.)

Situation 1b. Arrangement as in situation 1a but the subject is now asked to begin from the opposite end to the experimenter. (Distance moved, approximately 6 in.)

Situation 2. A_1C_1 and A_2C_2 are still parallel but A_2 is moved 10 cm or 4 in. to the left of A_1. The procedure of situation 1b is now repeated.

Situation 3. A_1C_1 still parallel to A_2C_2 and A_2 still 4 in. to left of A_1. Repeat procedure of 1a but experimenter to move his bead 15 in. i.e. longer than child's ruler.

Situation 4. Experimenter to use A_1C_1, subject to use A_3C_3. These to be parallel as before. Let A_3 be placed 4 in. to the right of A_1. Repeat procedure of 1b.

A 12-inch ruler, a piece of string, and length of manilla card were supplied for use by the subjects and were kept clearly in view beside lines A_1C_1, A_2C_2, and A_3C_3.

The stages of development described by Piaget are as follows:

Stage I: ⎫ Length of travel determined entirely by point of
Sub-stage IIA: ⎭ arrival. (Sample age 4:6–6:10 years.)

Sub-stage IIB: Intermediate responses: beginning to co-ordinate points of arrival with points of departure: beginning to understand the composition of segments: the beginnings of measurement. (Sample age 6:7–7:4 years.)

Sub-stage IIIA: Operational measurement but with only qualitative transitivity in the use of a common measure (i.e. the marking of the end points of measurement on material provided and transfer of this length in total, ignoring the use of the units marked on the ruler provided). (Sample age 7:10–8:7 years.)

Sub-stage IIIB: Operational measurement with unit iteration. (Sample age 7:11 onwards.)

Experiment 3. Locating a Point in Two Dimensions

Having studied the growth of measuring operations in one dimension this experiment allows us to consider that same development where two dimensions are involved.

The child is given two pieces of plain white paper identical in shape and size. The first, S_1, is placed at, and clipped to, the top right-hand corner of a piece of hardboard, the second, S_2, is similarly placed and clipped to the bottom left-hand corner (Fig. 3). The child is also provided with a ruler, cardboard strip, and a piece of string.

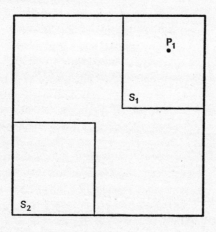

FIG. 3.

S_1 contains a point P_1 shown about half way between the centre of the sheet and its upper right-hand corner. The experimenter simply asks the subject to draw a point P_2 on the other sheet S_2, in exactly the same place as point P_1 on S_1. so that if the two sheets are superimposed P_2 will fall exactly over P_1. The paper used is semi-transparent writing paper and the subject can verify the coincidence of P_1 and P_2 by putting one sheet over the other.

When at the first attempt a child made only a visual estimate he was asked could he use any of the measuring material provided, and if he agreed that he could, was then encouraged to try again. After this attempt, if horizontal and vertical co-ordinates were not employed the child was asked would it help if the ruler, etc., was placed horizontally and vertically on the paper relative to the spot, and if he agreed it would, he was again encouraged to make a further attempt. If at any time in the experiment the child correctly located the point using either chance or measurement, two new sheets of paper were taken, a new spot sited on S_1, and the child reset the problem.

The stages of development described by Piaget are as follows:

Stage I:

Sub-stage IIA: The point P_2 is located visually. Measuring devices are either not used at all or are used perceptually and inappropriately. (Sample age 4:4–6:11 years.)

Sub stage IIB: Beginnings of measurement; measurement is one-dimensional. (Sample age 6:7–7:2 years.)

From Sub-stage IIB to sub-stage IIIA: Transition to two-dimensional measurement. (Sample age 5:8–7:2 years.)

Sub-stage IIIA: Empirical discovery of two-dimensional measurement; the result of trial and error. (Sample age 7:8–8:3 years.)

Sub-stage IIIB: Operational grasp of two-dimensional measurement; the use of horizontal and vertical co-ordinates. (Sample age 8:9 years onwards.)

Experiment 4. Measuring Angles

The child is shown a drawing of two supplementary angles *ADC* and *CDB* (Fig. 4) and is asked to make another drawing exactly similar. He is not permitted to look at the model while he is actually drawing, but he may study and measure it as often as he wishes while not actually engaged on his own drawing. This requirement is met quite simply by placing the model drawing on a desk behind the subject. Rulers, strips of paper, string, cardboard triangles (not fitting the angles), and compasses are provided for use. The inquiry is repeated three times in all, the drawing to copy being similar in each case, and after the first and

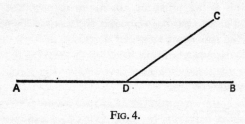

FIG. 4.

second attempts the child is questioned in such a way as to attract attention to the inaccuracies of his own drawing and suggest the further use of the rulers, etc., provided.

The stages of development described by Piaget are as follows:

Stage I ⎫ Visual judgement is used exclusively and the
       ⎬ lines are frequently drawn freehand. (Sample age
Sub-stage IIA: ⎭ up to 7:0 years.)

Sub-stage IIB: Measurement of lines commences and child attempts estimation of the angle, although this latter is still visual. (Sample age 7:3–7:7 years.)

Sub-stage IIIA: Subjects try to copy the slope, thus showing insight into parallelism, but they cannot measure angular separation. (Sample age 7:10–8:7 years.)

Sub-stage IIIB: Measurement of angular separation: *AC* or *CB*

(or both) is measured and used in addition to
the other measurements. (Sample age 8:6–9:10
years.)

Stage IV: Use of a right-angle in measuring angular separation—a perpendicular is drawn from *C* to *K*
on *ADB* and its measurements used. (Sample
age 10:4 onwards.)

Experiment 5. The Measurement of Areas, Unit Iteration

Unit iteration is that elementary form of measurement in
which a single unit is progressively placed in position, each
new position being adjacent to its preceding one, until an
entire length or area has been covered, the score of the positionings
needed for the task being recorded. Experiment 5 not only investigates the development of unit iteration in areas (as the title of the
experiment suggests) but also investigates the development of
the conservation of area.

The child is shown a number of shapes which are equal in area
but which differ markedly in shape. One (*A*) is a square which can
be composed out of nine smaller squares. The others (*B* and *C*)
are irregular figures made up of the same number of smaller
squares. The shapes are of plain card *without* the dotted lines
shown in Fig. 5.

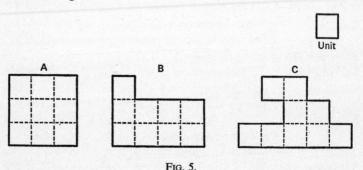

Fig. 5.

The child is given a cardboard square representing one unit, together with a pencil. He is free to examine the material and draw on it. He is asked the relationship of size between *A*, *B*, and *C*. If he does not know what to do, the experimenter shows him how to step the unit square, to cover the large square, by doing it for him two or three times, and telling him to carry on by himself. If the subject proves unable to draw in the squares the experimenter helps him to do so and the child is then asked if counting the squares would help. He is also asked which shape he would choose if they were made of chocolate.

On the completion of this problem the child is offered two heterogeneous shapes *D* and *E* cut out of plain card *without* the dotted lines shown in Fig. 6.

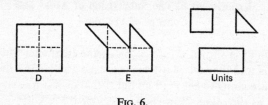

Fig. 6.

The child is offered a selection of units with which to measure these and is again asked to establish the size relationship between the given shapes. Where difficulty was experienced by the child the various measuring units were suggested in turn.

The stages of development described by Piaget are as follows:

Stage I: The child is unable to use the units at all and it is difficult to pursue the inquiry. (Sample age up to 4:11 years.)

Sub-stage IIA: The unit is used, but without transitivity. (Sample age 5:0–6:10 years.) ("Without transitivity" means without understanding that the unit may be moved across the given shape to measure size.)

Sub-stage IIB: Transitional; improved composition of sub-division but in the second problem the different-sized units are treated as equal, i.e. the notion of a metric unit is unformed. (Sample age 5:10–6:10 years.)

Sub-stage IIIA: The use of the common measure and the recognition of its transitivity are immediate, but unequal units are considered equal until the inequality is referred for the subject's attention. (Sample age 6:3–7:6 years.)

Sub-stage IIIB: Operational unit iteration. (Sample age 7:6–8:10 years.)

Experiment 6. The Subdivision of Areas and Concept of Fractions

The child is shown a disc of plasticine (diameter about 3 in.) and he is told that the plasticine is a cake and he and the experimenter are going to eat it all up but they must each have the same amount as the other. How shall we divide it? A knife is provided to cut the cake or he may divide it by laying on matchsticks which are also provided. When the problem of dichotomy has been solved (or attempted) a second "cake" is provided, and the subject is asked to divide this one totally and equally between his teacher, the experimenter, and himself. The child is also offered a paper circle, rectangle, and square, a pencil, and a pair of scissors. He is asked to divide and cut the paper shapes into thirds. Following the attempt at trichotomy the subject passes on to the problem of achieving quarters.

The stages of development described by Piaget are as follows:

Stage I: Problems of division into two equal parts (i.e. dichotomy). (General fragmentation attempted.) (Sample age up to 4:6 years.)

Sub-stage IIA: Can achieve dichotomy; problems of division into three equal parts (i.e. trichotomy). (Sample age 4:2–6 years.)

Sub-stage IIB: Successful trichotomy, gradual or by trial and error. (Sample age 6:0–7:0 years.)

Sub-stage IIIA: Immediate trichotomy. If the experiment is pursued as far as division into fifths and sixths, as it is by Piaget, there are at this stage problems of division into fifths and sixths. (Sample age 6:8–9:2 years.)

Sub-stage IIIB: Division into five or six equal parts. (Sample age 9:6 years onwards.)

CHAPTER 5

THE RESULTS OF THE SIX
EXPERIMENTS

AFTER the completion of each set of experiments each subject's completed protocol for the experiment (see Appendix 1) was compared with the salient features of each stage of development of the appropriate experiment, as recorded by Piaget in his book, and the performance placed provisionally in the appropriate stage. In five of the six experiments, protocols showing performance levels evenly balanced as transition from one stage to another occurred. In such cases it was decided to allocate a transition age, e.g. IIIA–IIIB. The stage allocated to each child in the sample of thirty for each experiment is shown in the table facing page 32.

The Results of Experiment 1. The Lengths of Lines and the Coincidence of Their Extremities (see protocols, p. 49)

Because of its simplicity the highest stage attainable in this experiment was stage IIB. Of the thirty children, twenty-three gave responses which were placed in that stage, the balance of seven were placed in stage IIA.

Of the seven placed in stage IIA there were two types. The first considered the plasticine snake and stick to be the same length until asked to run their hands along the two lengths, or consider the lengths that would have to be walked along them by two ants. A remarkable example of this type was Jacqueline. An examination of the table of results facing p. 32 will show that she did not achieve the stage expected for her age, etc., in this experiment, which one would have thought the simplest of the series given, and yet demonstrated a conservation of length and area in the others. Her individual histogram in Fig. 7 also shows this clearly. The second type stated in reply to the final question that the snake and the wood were the same length, having correctly described the disparity up to that point. It would seem to me this question is possibly misleading in that it seems to suggest that there is a "catch".

The children placed in stage IIB answered all the questions correctly.

The stages of development described by Piaget were found.

The Results of Experiment 2. Subdividing a Straight Line
(see protocols, p. 50)

The optimum stage in this experiment was IIIB and eight of the children achieved it. Notable amongst these was Robert, a first-year junior, who was the youngest placed at this stage, (see his histogram, Fig. 7) and it is only the A-stream children of the second and third years who do so well; not until the fourth year do we see B-stream children in the sample using unit iteration operationally.

Certain of the children in their responses showed the difficulty caused by a wide disparity between the result of their reasoning and the result of their visual perception. In consequence of this, these children's protocols show correct and incorrect solutions interspersed. George was a good example of a boy who, faced with a wide disparity, promptly discarded his thinking, and yet in subsequent experiments showed a high level of thinking. (See table facing p. 32.)

Jill, a first-year A-streamer, achieved correct results in each of the four situations in the experiments but relied entirely upon visual estimates of the distances. In consequence she was placed at stage IIB but subsequently, in a free classroom situation when engaged in knitting a set of doll's clothes, proved she was capable of good accurate measurements with a ruler without any teacher prompting. This suggests that she was not sufficiently interested in the experiment to take the trouble to use the ruler available, and so stage IIB is not the stage which her best motivated performance would earn her.

The patterns of response (and thus the stages of development) described by Piaget were very closely followed by the children in the sample.

The Results of Experiment 3. Locating a Point in Two Dimensions
(see protocols, p. 53)

The optimum stage was again IIIB and surprisingly both Robert and Ian, in the first-year A-stream, achieved this stage, and their performance is only equalled by the five children in the fourth year.

Piaget's patterns of response were largely followed by the children, although in the sample only one child measured diagonally from one corner, and no child attempted to hold the ruler angle steady while transferring it from S_1 to S_2 as described by Piaget (although in subsequent use of this experiment with children, other than those in the sample, this response has been observed). An interesting feature in the responses of the children who relied exclusively on visual estimate, was the astonishing accuracy with which they sited the point. Carol (age 7:2), in her first attempt, was about 1/10 in. incorrect, and in her second attempt with a new site, only about 1/8 in. out. Another interesting result was that of Jill, who, after the helpful question (c) suggesting the use of a horizontal and vertical measurement, proceeded to use the co-ordinates after a fashion, but when asked to repeat her performance with a new site, reverted to a single dimension—thus rejecting the advice offered, and advance shown previously, because she was not ready for it.

The developmental pattern shown supported that of Piaget's stages.

The Results of Experiment 4. Measuring Angles
(see protocols, p. 55)

The optimum stage for this experiment was stage IV and only two boys, Martin, a third-year A-streamer, and Kevin, a fourth-year C-streamer (!) achieved this. Alison (second-year A) produced an interesting solution in that she constructed a complete rectangle about the angle, the two long sides being ADB, the given base line, and a line parallel to it passing through C, the terminal point of the angle arm. By using the measurements of the two perpendiculars (the short sides of the rectangle) and the divided long side through C, the point C was correctly sited. She was not allocated stage IV, however, as she only achieved this solution after an initial attempt of lesser merit. Robert produced an interesting result in his ingenious use of the ruler as a form of protractor. (See page 56.)

The stages shown by the children were those described by Piaget.

The Results of Experiment 5. The Measurement of Areas—Unit Iteration (see protocols, p. 58)

Stage IIIB was the highest available in this experiment and it is remarkable that this was achieved by Jennifer, still in the infants' school. This stage was also achieved by Angela (first-year A) and Alison (second-year A), but all other children at this stage were in the third and fourth years of the junior school.

The stages of development were precisely as described by Piaget and the interesting feature was in the first question, answers to which repeatedly showed that the child only considered one dimension—the length of shape B—and on this based the assessment that B was larger.

As in experiment 2, certain of the children experienced the inner struggle between reasoning and visual perception. Edward is a good example of this, his perception of the apparent visual disparity outweighing his realization of the numerical identity. (See page 59.)

The Results of Experiment 6. The Subdivision of Areas and Concept of Fractions (see protocols, p. 62)

As this experiment was not pursued beyond the subdivision into halves, thirds, and quarters, the highest stage attainable was IIIA. Alison was the youngest child to attain this but the development through the chronological ages of the sample is actually the smoothest of the six experiments (see Fig. 9). The responses made by the children were very much in agreement with those recorded by Piaget, but it was difficult in a number of cases to allocate a stage, as a child would show different stages of development in the ability to subdivide a square and a circle. Piaget also records this difficulty, however.

The "perseveration" of a pattern of subdivision was a frequent feature when the child progressed from the trichotomy of a circle to that of a square (see Colin's protocol p. 66) and another fact that was well evidenced was that to a small child a "half" simply means a fragment, as indeed does a quarter (see Brian's protocol p. 62).

A Summary of the Results

In order that the results of the experiments may be considered in a comprehensive but summarized form they have been converted into three sets of graphs (Figs. 7, 8, and 9), the information for which has been drawn up in the table opposite.

In Fig. 7 an individual histogram, or "profile", of each child's performance has been drawn on a single sheet. The comparative performance for each child in each experiment may be clearly seen and the "average stage" of development is stated at the base of each child's "block". The lower level of what Piaget classifies

The Experiments—Results Tabulated in Piagetian Stages

Name	School "stream"	Age years: months	Experiment 1	Experiment 2	Experiment 3	Experiment 4	Experiment 5	Experiment 6	"Average" stage
Katherine	B	5:10	IIB	I–IIA	IIA	I–IIA	I	I	I–IIA
Graham	B	6:3	IIB	I–IIA	I	I–IIA	I	IIA	I–IIA
Stephen	A	6:3	IIB	I–IIA	IIA	I–IIA	I	IIA	IIA
Lynne	A	6:3	IIB	IIB	I	I–IIA	IIB	IIA	IIA–IIB
Janet	C	6:4	IIA	I–IIA	I	I–IIA	I–IIA	IIA	I–IIA
Brian	B	6:5	IIA	IIA–IIB	I–IIA	I–IIA	I	I	I–IIA
Carol	A	7:2	IIB	I–IIA	IIA	I–IIA	IIB	IIA	IIA–IIB
Pat	B	7:3	IIB	IIA–IIB	I	I–IIA	IIA	IIA	IIA
Michael	C	7:4	IIB	I–IIA	I	I–IIA	I–IIA	IIA	I–IIA
Jennifer	A	7:5	IIA	IIB	IIB	IIB–IIIA	IIIB	IIB–IIIA	IIB–IIIA
Edward	B	7:10	IIB	I–IIA	I–IIA	I–IIA	IIA	IIB	IIA
Jill	A	8:0	IIB	IIB	IIB	IIB	IIB	IIB	IIB
Robert	A	8:1	IIB	IIIB	IIIB	IIIA	IIB	IIB	IIIA
Ian	A	8:1	IIB	IIIA	IIIB	IIB	IIB	IIA	IIB–IIIA
Angela	A	8:6	IIA	IIA–IIB	IIIA	IIB	IIIB	IIB	IIB–IIIA
Anthony	B	8:7	IIB	I–IIA	IIB	IIB	IIB	IIA–IIB	IIA–IIB
Alison	A	8:10	IIB	IIIB	IIIA	IIIB	IIIB	IIIA	IIIA–IIIB
John	A	9:0	IIB	IIIB	IIIA	IIIA–IIIB	IIB	IIA–IIB	IIB–IIIA
Irene	B	9:1	IIA	IIB	IIIA–IIIB	IIA–IIB	IIB	IIB	IIB
Richard	C	9:2	IIB	I–IIA	IIA	I–IIA	IIA	IIB	IIA
Leslie	B	9:7	IIA	IIB	IIIA	IIB	IIIA	IIB	IIB
Linda	A	9:10	IIB	IIIB	IIIA	IIIA–IIIB	IIIB	IIIA	IIIA–IIIB
Martin	A	9:10	IIB	IIIB	IIIA	IV	IIIB	IIB–IIIA	IIIA–IIIB
Jacqueline	B	9:11	IIA	IIB	IIIA	IIIB	IIIB	IIIA	IIIA
Gladys	C	10:3	IIB	IIB	IIA	IIB	IIIA	IIB	IIB
Mary	B	10:6	IIB	IIIB	IIIB	IIB	IIB	IIIA	IIIA
Colin	A	10:9	IIB	IIIB	IIIB	IIIB	IIIB	IIIA	IIIA–IIIB
George	B	10:11	IIB	I–IIA	IIIB	IIIB	IIIB	IIIA	IIIA
Kevin	C	11:1	IIB	I–IIA	IIIB	IV	IIIB	IIIA	IIIA
Audrey	A	11:5	IIB	IIIB	IIIB	IIIB	IIIB	IIIA	IIIA–IIIB

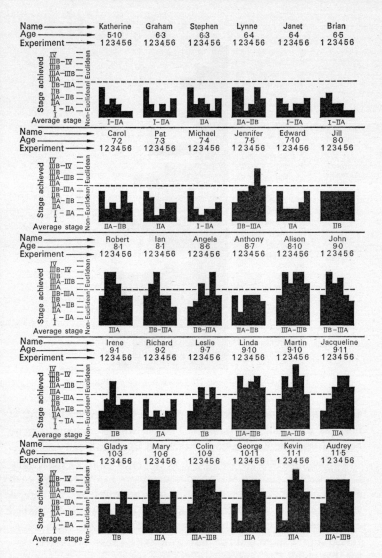

FIG. 7. Individual histograms.

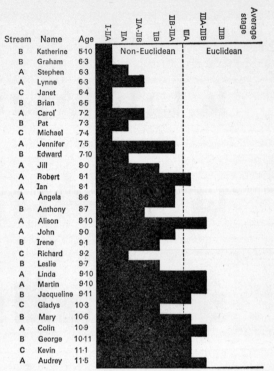

FIG. 8. Histogram showing each child's average stage.

as "Euclidean constructions of space" is indicated by the dotted line on this multiple graph. Children whose columns extend beyond this line have begun to develop Euclidean constructions.

To facilitate the allocation of an average stage to each child in the sample, the ten stages and sub-stages available were each given a "score" of from 1 to 10, from the lowest to the highest stage. A child's total score on the six experiments was then totalled and divided by six, the resulting average score was then reconverted into a stage and this has been named the "average stage" for that child. The fault inherent in this system lies in the fact that only in Experiment 4 was stage IV attainable, in Experiment 6 stage IIIA was the optimum level, and in Experiment 1 no child could do better than stage IIB because of the limitations of the experiment.

It should be remembered then, that what in Fig. 8 is labelled the child's "average stage", is really a stage representative of his performance in these six experiments with their several limitations. The value of this histogram lies in its increased simplicity over Fig. 7 and it presents an immediate pictorial comparison of each child's overall representative performance.

The set of six graphs presented in Fig. 9 is designed to compare the developmental stage for each child with the increasing age of each child. The information for these graphs is drawn from the table facing p. 32 and allows an easy comparison to be made between the patterns of performance and age in each experiment. In each graph the dotted line represents the age of each child as named at the foot of the set of graphs; the unbroken line represents the stage achieved in the experiment. If the development stage was entirely dependent upon chronological age, then, we could expect the two lines to be parallel in each case. However, the stage of development is also dependent upon intelligence, and since we have children drawn from A, B, and C streams of primary schools in the sample, we must expect a "scatter" of results about the chronological graph, which, after a fashion, is achieved. Special experience and teaching, however, are also factors which will affect the behaviour of the unbroken line, the former possibly increasing the range of the scatter, especially in the younger age range, the latter probably decreasing the scatter, especially in the upper two years of the age range.

This, then, completes a simple consideration of the results recorded in the carrying out of these six experiments with a sample of English children. This is, of course, only a tiny follow-up study of some of Piaget's experimental work but the interested reader can find accounts of others. Two of particular interest are those conducted by Lovell and Ogilvie,[7] and by Lunzer,[8] as they investigated another section of the work described in *The Child's Conception of Geometry* (from which the

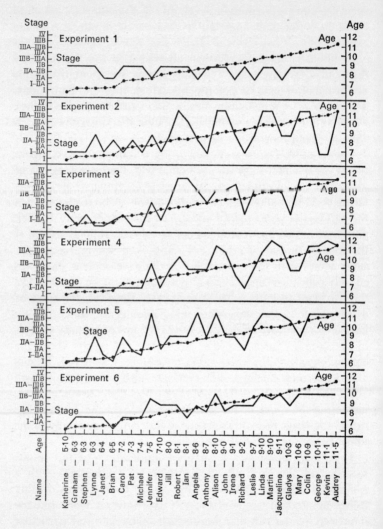

FIG. 9. Graphs comparing stages of development with chronological ages.

six experiments above were taken)—that of Piaget's treatment of volume. Both studies confirm the Piagetian sequence of stages of development, but Lovell and Ogilvie find some modification of the development within the states, and state that more is assumed from a single experiment by Piaget than is justifiable in the light of the results of his experiments. Lunzer, on the other hand, states that from his experimental results "the dependence of displacement volume and mathematical multiplication in geometry, on the notions of infinity and continuity, is certainly called into serious jeopardy". Also he states that another developmental factor neglected by Piaget is that "very few could arrive by themselves at a valid method of calculating volume in the absence of geometrical teaching—which takes place at 12 or 13". The criticisms implicit in these statements have, of course, been made by others and may be added to those considered in Chapter 7.

CHAPTER 6

THE RESULTS OF THE EXPERIMENTS INTERPRETED

It is of interest to note that the children in the sample from the junior classes all had ruler and geometrical drawing lessons each week, working to a scheme of work prescribed by the LEA. The infants in the sample, of course, did not have this, but did have free number activity when they would frequently measure in the pursuit of their own interests.

From such a small sample as five in each year in the infant and junior course, it is naturally impossible to justify the drawing of definite conclusions. However, it is possible to consider the "indications" pointed by the results, bearing in mind the limitations which are compulsorily imposed. These indications, although requiring far more corroboration than this study, would seem to be worth thought.

The Indications of the Results

(a) The stages of development as described by Piaget (in these experiments) were corroborated by the children's replies and responses in each of the six experiments.

(b) The level of development shown by a child is not necessarily the optimum. Jill's difference in performance in the free classroom situation and in Experiment 2 indicate this. Among the very young children there were also several instances of their performance being possibly adversely affected by emotional factors, resulting from "not being able to do it". Both Brian and Katherine were affected by this in Experiments 5 and 6.

(c) Where the experimenter offered helpful advice in the course of the experiment it would only be accepted and used by those who were "ready" for it. A child not ready for it would discard such advice. This was shown on several occasions but in particular by Jill in Experiment 3, who, when asked the helpful question (c) agreed that it would help, but ignored the suggestion and did not act upon it.

(d) From Fig. 7. In all the individual profiles except one, different levels of development are apparent in each child. Kevin and George show the full range from stage I–IIA to stage IV, having both been misled by the apparent visual disparity in Experiment 2. The presence of these various levels in each child must affect the teaching and learning situation.

(e) From Fig. 8. A fairly steady rise up to the optimum average stage possible (IIIA–IIIB) appears, if one remembers that Anthony, Irene, and Leslie are B-stream children and Richard and Gladys C-stream children. In the third and fourth year, only Leslie and Gladys, in classes IIIB and C respectively, failed to achieve a general level of Euclidean constructions. The teaching factor must be considered as at least an assistant force here.

(f) From Fig. 9. Each experiment shows a scatter of the development stages about the chronological age graph (again remembering that there are A, B, and C-stream children in the sample). The individual differences between different children in the same class, while performing the same experiment, can be clearly seen, e.g. Mary and George in Experiment 2; Jennifer and Michael in Experiment 5. These differences are another factor to be borne in mind in the teaching and learning situations.

Experiment 6 shows the closest scatter about the age line, and despite the limitations upon the drawing of conclusions imposed by the small sample, and the slight confinement of scatter resulting from the optimum stage being only IIIA, it is interesting to consider that of the six experiments possibly none could be influenced more by special experience and teaching than this one. All children see cakes cut and divided, and it is a common act for a junior school child to share out a bar of chocolate amongst friends, or divide up a circular "wheel" of confectionery. In addition, the cutting up of paper shapes into fractions is a common activity in the junior school.

(g) In a comparison of the ages at which each level of development may be expected, according to Piaget, and those at which the levels were discovered in these experiments, it would seem that the children in the sample were rather slower than those in Piaget's book. The disparity is not large—an average of 6–7 months probably. A possible explanation for this fact is that the intelligence range of both the English schools used was rather "flat-topped"—had a full range of intelligence at the high level been present, the average age of incidence of levels of development would probably have been lower, and thus nearer to those given by Piaget (who does not, by the way, describe the selection procedure and constitution of his sample).

From a consideration of the results of the experiments and their indications, together with careful character studies of a number of the children included in the sample, certain general factors which affect the learning and teaching situations are suggested. These are stated below.

1. FACTORS WHICH AFFECT THE LEARNING SITUATION

(a) Maturation

The importance of maturation in concept development was was clearly illustrated by the results of the experiments. Figure 8 on p. 34 shows the simple progression of performance that age brings (making allowance for the range of intelligence in the sample). Inextricably linked with maturation too is the accumulation of experience, both general and specific, which comes with the passing of time, and this also greatly assists concept development.

Nor must the effect of the great range of maturation one finds in a single chronological age group be overlooked.

(b) The individual differences between children

Children are individuals—not groups or classes. Within a single chronological group they will differ, as just stated, in maturation, and also in economic circumstances, in moral backgrounds, in a thousand and one different ways physically, socially, emotionally, intellectually, and in experience, one from another. And as they differ so will their level of learning vary.

(c) There are great differences in the general and specific experiences of children

To illustrate this point let us consider that quite obviously the range of employment of the parents will introduce, at second hand, differences in experience for the children; the range of the parents' interests will again extend these differences. Robert, the 8-year-old boy in the sample, was interested in all mechanical matters and had experience and knowledge of them because he was close to his father, who was a maintenance engineer in a local factory. He had talked to Robert, shown him around the factory, and introduced him to his interests. The other children of his age group in the sample did not have this experience, but nevertheless had something from their parents and family circle that Robert did not have. This simple illustration may be extended a thousand-fold, and children use their different individual experiences in their learning processes.

From a consideration of Fig. 8 on p. 34 it is evident that Euclidean concepts of measurement may generally be expected to appear at about the third year in the junior school stage, but since experience, both general and specific, affects the learning situation so vitally, there is reason to believe that specific experience in measurement, or lack of it, could advance, or delay, the development of this concept (and a similar statement could probably be made about the growth of any other concept). As was stated at the beginning of this chapter, all the junior children in the sample followed the LEA's scheme of ruler drawing and measurement, and so had the same directed specific experience of it.

(d) The "whole" child is involved in the learning process

The child does not learn only through his intellectual ability. Involved in his learning process are his emotions, his degree of motivation, and, as already stated, his store of previous experience. A child may be restricted in development in some way at home, as Ian, in the sample, was restricted emotionally and socially, and this will and did affect his conduct and behaviour at school, and his standard of attainment and efficiency in the learning situation. Jill showed a lack of motivation in Experiment 2 when she refused to use the ruler provided, but when sufficiently motivated showed a higher level of development and ability by measuring her knitting (p. 29). Robert was undoubtedly helped to produce his consistently high-standard results in his school work by the social prestige and self-confidence his athletic prowess brought him.

These are three very simple single illustrations of a very complex situation which can only be expressed in the phrase—the "whole" child is involved in the learning process.

2. FACTORS WHICH AFFECT THE TEACHING SITUATION

(a) The child needs to be "ready" for the teaching

For the child to gain full and lasting benefit from teaching it is necessary for him to be "ready" for it—ready in every way, emotionally, socially, physically, in experience, and intellectually. Only if this full readiness is present is the full value of the teaching absorbed. This point was apparent several times in Experiments 3 and 5 when the child was advised helpfully by the experimenter, but discarded the advice unless ready for it. As has been stated, Jill was a clear example of this.

This matter, of course, is one involving the skill of the teacher, who must detect when the child is ready, and also know in advance the skill and ability the child must have to be ready.

(b) Partial ability will precede the full concept

As already stated, the Euclidean concept of measurement seems to appear generally at about the age of 9 or 10 years, but many children who have not achieved the full Euclidean concept demonstrated a definite competency. Such ability comes through accumulative maturation and experience, and is naturally to be expected to precede the full ability. It is essential to exercise such partial abilities to assist them in their growth, but nevertheless recognize them as partial and not comprehensive.

(c) Verbal and formal teaching have little place in the primary school

Throughout the 180 experiments recorded in Chapters 4 and 5 the children were observed to rely upon visual perception and concrete operations to solve the problems posed. Only the cleverest children in the oldest age group generally showed formal reasoning, and so these results would strongly support the theory that the primary school child bases his thinking on what he sees and what he does. It is necessary, therefore, for the school to plan first-hand experiences for the child so that what he sees and does is of the maximum benefit to him; the school must provide for ample opportunity for the right experiences to be gained by directed and undirected activity, and must be forever on its guard that it does not, by over direction, positively prevent the gaining of such experience.

(d) A framework of development and progression is needed in the planned work

Contemporary educational thought advocates for each teacher, class, and child the maximum freedom possible from the limiting and narrowing influence of a rigid syllabus. It is believed that with such freedom comes the greatest opportunity to benefit from the educational sources located in the environment, and in the knowledge, experience, enthusiasm, and interests of the teachers, and the interests and experiences of the children as they naturally develop.

This is surely true, but the main problem for the practising teacher, who holds this belief, is to plan for, and hold within his mind, the overall scheme of conceptual progression for the child. This is not an easy matter for the teacher who places his children in an environment of integrated activity and experience, as those who have tried it have found out for themselves. However, this is a situation where the patterns of concept development found by Piaget can be of immense practical value. The Nuffield approach to the teaching of mathematics and science very carefully considers and adapts the Piagetian patterns, and this is surely only the beginning of a comprehensive practical use of Jean Piaget's work.

CHAPTER 7

A BRIEF CRITICAL REVIEW AND CONSIDERATION OF PIAGET'S THEORIES

As HAS been stated on p. 3 of this book, Piaget seldom defines his terms but he does give us his definition of intelligence.[10] This seems a very good starting point for a critical consideration of Piaget's theories.

In 1921 the editor of the *Journal of Educational Psychology* invited seventeen psychologists to take part in a symposium. Contributors were asked to answer two questions, the first of which was a request for a definition of their concept of intelligence. Fourteen psychologists replied with fourteen different answers, and this result, plus the undoubted difficulty involved, has possibly given rise to the opinion held by some that "many definitions of what is really indefinable have been attempted by psychologists and that intelligence is still indefinable". Nevertheless, despite this possibility, every effort at a definition is valuable as it helps to clear and to discipline thought on the subject—and there is no lack of attempts.

When considering the multiplicity of definitions, Vernon[13] comments upon the large central area of overlap shown in almost all of them, and it seems within this large area of overlap, not only of the symposium definitions, but of many others too, that Knight has built his definition. He suggests that

> Intelligence is the ability when we have some aim or question in mind (a) to discover the relevant qualities and relations of the objects or ideas that are before us, and (b) to evoke other relevant ideas. In other words

45

it is the capacity for relational constructive thinking, directed to the attainment of some end.[5]

Piaget defines intelligence as "the state of equilibrium towards which tend all the successive adaptations of a sensori-motor and cognitive nature, as well as all assimilatory and accommodatory interactions between the organism and the environment". The important term for us in this definition is "equilibrium". As he states that "reversibility" is the very criterion of equilibrium, it follows that Piaget considers intelligence in terms of the ability to achieve reversibility in reasoning, when dealing with the "mobile structures" presented by the world to the human organism. To achieve "reversibility" it is imperative "to discover the relevant qualities and relations of the objects or ideas that are before us" and to achieve progressive equilibrium it is certainly necessary "to evoke other relevant ideas". It would seem, then, that in this matter of definition, Piaget, when he talks about intelligence, although using a vastly different phraseology and technology, is nevertheless remarkably in accord with Knight, and hence with that large central area of overlap of definition mentioned by Vernon. From this, then, we may say that when Piaget talks about intelligence he means the same as his contemporaries—there can be little adverse criticism in this section of his theory.

Let us now consider some recorded criticisms of Piaget's methods and maturation system. At the same time as the first section of Piaget's work (1925–32), Susan Isaacs was carrying out her experimental work in the Malting House School. Her plan was to have the children under continual observation, and this was the great difference between her approach and Piaget's—she observed the "whole" child in an unstructured situation, and she was keenly critical of Piaget in two matters in particular. Firstly, Susan Isaacs[4] stated that the differences between her conclusions and his were that he attributed "to maturation certain phenomena which can be shown to be, to a real extent, a function of experience", and secondly, that from the observations she made of the development of the children in her school her "records as a whole cut right across any hard-and-fast notion of mental "structures". . . . They show rather a continuous advance in scope and clarity . . . and in the ability to handle experience in more and more complex forms".

"Intellectual growth", she stated, "certainly shows a psychological coherence; but this coherence has the elasticity and vital movement of a living process, not the rigid formality of a logical system . . . and will be affected by all of those psychological influences to which each child is prone". These were sweeping criticisims and opposing ideas.

It is significant, that in the second period of his work, which began in 1936, Piaget very considerably changed his approach and, as has been stated on p. 14, far less criticism resulted. However, there have been criticisms of this period too; this was inevitable, but it is now much more frequently mingled with admiration, and far less often with detraction. Thomson[12] states that "one of the criticisms directed against Piaget is that his researches into the origin and development of thought in children do not pay sufficient attention to the factor of learning". This would seem to be a legitimate observation, for quite apart from the development of the ability to perform the sort of operation that Piaget studies in his experiments, the child also acquires the capacity to learn, and of course he does learn, both from general and specific experience. This is affirmed also by Lovell.[6] "The growth of these concepts is much more complex than Piaget allows, and depends much more on the experience of the physical world, and of working with many different media in many situations, than he suggests". Lovell's evidence for this lies in his follow-up studies to Piaget's work, which show the value especially of specific experience.

The "system" developed by Piaget is too rigid. Despite the development of his work, this criticism by Susan Isaacs still applies to a certain degree, though not as comprehensively now, as when Susan Isaacs first published her findings over 30 years ago. The "system" still does not allow for the fact that due to specific experience, motivation, the circumstances of the moment, and other factors, a child's thought functions at many different levels.

The system is also too general, for a certain specificity in the development of the stages occurs—for example spatial relations are mastered usually at a much earlier age than are the relations of time.

Finally, in this matter of general criticism, the structured situation of Piaget's experiments has been greatly improved in the second period of his work, but is still not ideal. It cannot be, for it *is* "structured" and artificial, and can offer no complete assurance that what is observed is the "real" level of the child's development in a natural situation—it can only show the level of development in the particular experimental situation being studied. This fact must be borne in mind when considering the evidence furnished by the Piagetian experiment; but in its favour it must be stated that it is invaluable, and so far unique, in the opportunity for discovery and study of the various stages of development that it affords to the researcher and to the ordinary teacher.

These, then, are some general criticisms of Piaget's theories as stated by a representational few of his contemporaries among educational thinkers. As a practising teacher, concerned intimately with the learning and teaching situation, my observations and interpretations of the results of the six experiments, as recorded in Chapter 6, contain inevitably a criticism of the Piagetian "system". A rereading of Chapter 6 will suggest repeatedly that his too rigid system should be modified into a more flexible form to allow for factors apparently disregarded by Piaget, factors such as experience, specific and general, such as the motivation of the child, and such as the teaching factor. But my concluding thought is this: with all the legitimate criticisms one must allow with regard to his work and theories, we are only beginning to assess the debt we shall owe to Piaget, for he has already enabled us to observe and find out so much more than we previously knew about the way children think and learn. It is surely significant that with the passing of each year the current of criticism of his work grows ever weaker, and the tide of appreciation and praise ever stronger.

SELECTED PROTOCOLS FOR EACH STAGE
OF EACH EXPERIMENT

FOR the first example of each experiment a complete protocol is given; in each subsequent protocol, in each experiment, the descriptive sections of the protocol are entirely omitted, and the questions asked by the investigator are given simply as the number shown on the original protocol. The child's reply and action are given and described in full.

A. Experiment 1. The Length of Lines and the Coincidence of their Extremities

Leslie   **Sub-stage IIA**   **9 years 7 months**

Child is given a 10 cm rod of wood and a longer undulating thread made of plasticine and shaped like a "snake". The ends of the plasticine are made to coincide with those of the wooden rod. (See p. 18, Fig. 1.)

1. Say "Are they the same length [pointing only], or is one longer than the other?"
   "Why?"

   Recorded reply. "They're the same." "Because they're as long as each other."

2. If the child says "same length", ask him to run his hands along the stick and "snake" and repeat question 1.

   Recorded reply. "They're as long as each other."

3. If he persists in "same length" ask him if ants or little men walked along the lines would they find one longer than the other?

   Recorded reply. "The plasticine is longer than the other, I think."

4. "Snake" is now straightened.
   Say "Are they the same length [pointing only], or is one longer than the other?"
   "Why?"

   Recorded reply. "The plasticine is longer." "I can see it is."

5. Twist "snake" back to original shape and repeat question 1.

   Recorded reply. "Now they're the same length."

   Comment. Subject thinks curvilinear shape is longer after suggestion of movement, but reverts to original judgement after further static inspection.

Jennifer	Sub-stage IIA	7 years 5 months

1. *Recorded reply.* "That one is longer than that one." (Plasticine longer than wood.)
   "Because that one's creased up and that one's straight."

2 and 3. Not applicable.

4. "That one's longer than that one." (Pointing to plasticine as longer.)
   "Because it's bigger."

5. (After a longish pause.) "I think they're the same size just now, because it doesn't stick out now its curled up."

   Comment. Intermediate responses, allocation of sub-stage IIA resulting from answer to question 5. (But was Jennifer misled by easiness of experiment and question, into thinking there was a "catch" and thus not answering what she really thought?)

Lynne	Sub-stage IIB	6 years 3 months

1. *Recorded reply.* "One is longer than the other—the plasticine." "Because you can bend your finger on it." Demonstrates meaning by laying bent forefinger on a bend in the plasticine.

2 and 3. Not applicable.

4. "Because there's a lot of plasticine here." Points to ends of straightened plasticine projecting past stick.

5. "The plasticine is still longer."

   Comment. Length is differentiated from the simple consideration of the end points.

B. Experiment 2. Subdividing a Straight Line

George	Stage I–IIA	10 years 11 months

   Materials. In addition to the pieces of wood, a ruler, piece of string, and length of manilla card are provided.

1(a) Two wires, A_1C_1, A_2C_2, which are equal in length, are placed parallel to one another with their ends in alignment, A_1 opposite A_2. (See p. 19, Fig. 2.) Say, "The bead is a train travelling along a railway line. My bead [train] is going this far [experimenter moves his bead 6 in. from A_1: i.e. a distance shorter than the child's ruler]. I want you to make your bead [train] do a journey that is just as long as mine; one the same length. Start your bead from here[A_2]."
Pause. "Where will you go?" "How can you be sure?" See that the ruler, string, and manilla are clearly in view.

> *Recorded actions and comments.* Moves B_2 and sites it visually level with B_1. Is asked, "How can you be sure?" Reply. "Measure it." He does so and makes A_2B_2 equal A_1B_1.

(b) Repeat procedure 1(a) but the subject is now asked to move his bead from the other end, i.e. C_2.

> *Recorded actions and comments.* Measures A_1B_1 and starts to measure from C_2. Stops measuring and moves B_2 level with B_1 so that A_2B_2 equals A_1B_1 (not C_2B_2 equalling A_1B_1 as would be correct).

2. A_1C_1 and A_2C_2 still parallel but A_2 is moved 10 cm or about 4 in. to the left of A_1. Repeat procedure of 1(b).

> *Recorded actions and comments.* Does not measure, simply lines up B_2 level with B_1 (only interested in point of arrival).

3. A_1C_1 still parallel to A_2C_2, and A_2 still 4 in. to left of A_1. Repeat procedure of 1(a) but experimenter to move his bead 15 in., i.e. longer than the child's ruler.

> *Recorded actions and comments.* Again simply lines up B_2 with B_1.

4. Experimenter to use A_1C_1, subject to use A_3C_3 (longer than A_1C_1). These to be parallel as before. Let A_3 be placed 4 in. to the right of A_1. Repeat procedure of 1(b).

> *Recorded actions and comments.* Lines up B_3 with B_1 regardless of distance of travel. (Only concerned with point of arrival.)

At each stage of the experiment the subject is asked:
"Where will your bead go?"
"How can you be sure?" or, "How do you know that you are right?"

Comment. Length of travel is determined entirely by point of arrival.

Jill   **Sub-stage IIB**   **8 years 0 months**

1(a) Moves bead to correct position by visual estimate. Is asked, "How can you be sure you're right?" Answers, "Because I can see I'm right from here."

(b)   Moves bead by visual estimate so that A_1B_1 equals C_2B_2. Is again asked, "How can you be sure you're right?" Makes no attempt to use any of the measuring equipment right beside her, replies, "It's right because it looks the same."

2.   Moves bead by visual estimate so that A_1B_1 equals C_2B_2. Is sure she is right because, "If I turned my stick around then my bead would be level with yours."

3.   Again places bead visually in approximately correct position. "I know it's right because this distance [B_1C_1 is indicated by pointing] looks the same as this distance." (B_2C_2 indicated.)

4.   Bead again placed in approximately correct position by visual estimate. Subject states, "It is right because it looks right."

       Comment. Approximately correct solutions found in each question but visual estimate used exclusively.

Ian   **Sub-stage IIIA**   **8 years 1 month**

1(a)   Moves bead to approximately correct position. Asked, "How can you be sure?" Replies, "By measuring." Takes ruler and lays it *across* the wires parallel with the ends of the wooden mounting lengths (i.e. the ruler is not used as a measuring device but as an aid to perception).

 (b)   Measures A_1B_1, marks length on ruler with finger; uses this to measure B_2 the correct distance from C_2. Is sure he is right because, "I measured it."

2.   Using strip of manilla card measures A_1B_1 and places B_2 so that C_2B_2 is equal in length. Then takes ruler and checks the two distances to ensure his card measurement was correct.

3.   Using card strip and ruler, end to end, marks off on card the extra length needed to add to the ruler to give A_1B_1. Using this end-to-end technique the equal distance A_2B_2 is measured and B_2 correctly placed. Measurements are now checked by measuring B_1C_1 and B_2C_2 and ensuring their equality on the ruler.

4.   Commences measurement of A_1B_1 with finger span plus finger breadth. Using this system of measurement places B_3 so that A_1B_1 equals C_3B_3. Both distances are now measured by means of ruler and C_3B_3 adjusted to correct length. "I know I'm right because I measured it roughly with my fingers first, and then measured it 'right' with the ruler."

       Comment. Operational measurement but with only qualitative transitivity in the use of a common measure.

| Mary | Sub-stage IIIB | 10 years 6 months |

1(a) Moves B_2 level with B_1. Is asked "How can you be sure?" Takes ruler and measures and corrects so that A_1B_1 is exactly equalled by A_2B_2.

(b) Using ruler measures A_1B_1 and sets C_2B_2 to equal it.

2. Using ruler measures A_1B_1 and sets C_2B_2 to equal it.

3. Measures A_1B_1 using ruler and part of ruler again. Lays off this distance accurately, again using length of ruler and part of length again. A_1B_1 equals A_2B_2.

4. Measures A_1B_1 and places B_3 so that C_3B_3 is equal to it using the ruler to measure accurately.

Comment. Operational measurement with unit iteration.

C. Experiment 3. Locating a Point in Two Dimensions

| Stephen | Sub-stage IIA | 6 years 3 months |

Materials. A sheet of paper is fastened to the top right-hand corner of a sheet of hardboard. Towards the right-hand corner of the paper a red dot is made. The child is given another similar sheet of paper in the left-hand corner of the piece of hardboard. (See p. 21, Fig. 3.) Ruler, cardboard strip, piece of string.

1(a) Say, "I want you to make a large dot on this piece of paper [pointing] in exactly the same place as this one on this sheet [pointing]. If we put your piece of paper [pointing] on this piece [pointing] your dot should be on top of this one." Record actions and any reply.

Places dot by visual estimate in approximately the right place.

Note if child measures from bottom left or top right-hand corner. If he makes an attempt to place a dot on his piece of paper say, "Let's see if that's right", and place over the other piece. Record child's comment and reply.

Notes his error in silence.

(b) Say, "Could you use this ruler, piece of cardboard, string, or your hand to help you?" (Is given clean sheet of paper.) Record action and reply.

Again places dot by visual estimate. Is almost exactly correct.

Note if he measures from bottom left or top right-hand corner. Place piece of paper over top sheet whenever necessary.

(c) Say, "Would it help if you placed the ruler [or whatever he fancies] along this way [horizontal] or this way [vertical]?" Give a further clean sheet of paper. Record actions and reply.

Nods his head. Lays ruler obliquely from spot on top sheet S_1 to own paper S_2 and marks his spot at the end of the ruler.

Note the corner the child measures from.

(d) In the case of a child who has located the point, whether by chance or by proper measurement, make a new dot on the top right-hand sheet and ask him to make a dot on a clean bottom sheet to tally with this. Record actions and reply.
Not applicable.

    Comment. An example of a child at the upper end of the Stage I-IIA. The point is located visually, measuring device used perceptually.

Jill	Sub-stage IIB	8 years 0 months

1(a) Places dot entirely by visual estimate. On checking correctness by superimposition states, "Mine's too far down."

(b) Takes ruler and places it horizontally on own paper from right-hand edge and again visually estimates location of dot. On again superimposing S_1 and S_2 says, "Now it's a bit higher up."

(c) "Yes". Takes ruler and measures vertically from top of S_1 and horizontally from right-hand edge. Lays off these measurements on S_2 and approximately locates dot. Is not quite correct because on S_2 ruler was not held accurately at 90 degrees to the paper's edge.

(d) Measures horizontally from right-hand edge and vertically from top of S_1. Only transfers the single horizontal measurement. Makes visual estimate for depth of dot from top of S_2. Location of dot is too high.
    Comment. Measurement is still one-dimensional.

Alison	Sub-stage IIIA	8 years 10 months

1(a) Measures with ruler diagonally from top right-hand corner of S_1 to dot. Lays off this measurement on S_2, adjusting ruler by visual estimate for correct angle. (No attempt was made to preserve angle of ruler on transfer from S_1 to S_2.) S_1 and S_2 compared. Child smiles but makes no comment.

(b) Begins to repeat process of 1(a), stops to think, shakes head. Marks diagonal line from dot on S_1 to corner of paper S_1 with thumb nail. Experimentally tries horizontal measurement along top edge of S_1 and then approximately vertical measurement on S_1. Lays off these measurements on S_2 and sites dot. Dot is correct.

(c) Not applicable.

(d) Using ruler on S_1 measures horizontal distance from dot to right-hand edge of paper. Draws freehand pencil line from dot to right-hand edge of paper. Measures vertical depth, from corner, of terminal point of this pencil line. These two measurements now laid off on S_2. Dot located correctly.

    Comment. Good example of empirical discovery of two-dimensional measurement.

Robert   **Sub-stage IIIB**   **8 years 1 month**

1(a)   Measures vertical and horizontal distance of dot from top and right-hand edge of S_1, marking the distances on his ruler. Using these measurements locates point correctly on own paper without hesitation. When S_2 is superimposed on S_1, and correctness of location of dot on S_2 thus demonstrated, grins happily.

(b) and (c)   Not applicable.

(d)   Repeats performance as in 1(a). When correctness is again demonstrated by superimposition says, "I knew it was right because I measured how far in it was, and how far down, and then I did it on my own paper."

     Comment. Operational grasp of two-dimensional measurement.

D. Experiment 4. The Measurement of Angles

Edward   **Sub-stage I–IIA**   **7 years 10 months**

     Materials. Drawing of two supplementary angles. (See p. 23, Fig. 4). Paper, rulers, string, cardboard triangle, compasses, strips of manilla card.

     Procedure. Place the drawing on a chair behind the child. The piece of paper on which he must make a drawing exactly similar, is placed on a table in front of the child. The child may study and measure the model in any way he likes, and as often as he likes while not actually engaged on his drawing.

1(a)   Say, "Look at this drawing [no. 1]. I want you to make one just like it on this piece of paper." Record comments and actions.
Both *AB* and *DC* drawn freehand after briefest of examination of drawing (no. 1).

(b)   Say, "If there is anything you want to help, use whatever you can find on the table." Record comments and actions.
Says nothing. Makes second drawing as in 1(a).

(c)   Here are some typical promptings:
       (i)   "Do you need a ruler?"
       (ii)   "What do you need to make it just right?"
       (iii)   "Is there anything else you ought to measure?"
       (iv)   "Can you correct this?"
       (v)   "Why is your drawing not right?"
       (vi)   "How did you find that point *K*?" (Fig. 12, p. 58.)
       (vii)   "Why did you need point *K*?"
Record actions and comments.
Prompt no. (i) asked. Replies, "No." Child then asked, "Is your drawing exactly right?" Replies, "I think so."

     Comment. Visual judgement used exclusively.

Gladys   **Sub-stage IIB**   **10 years 3 months**

1(a) Measures *AB* with ruler. Draws *AB* on paper. Measures *DC* with ruler. Draws *DC* estimating visually the position of *D* at first, then correcting by measuring *AD* and drawing in *DC* again. Angle *BDC* not measured but drawn by visual estimate.

(b) Not applicable—child already using equipment provided.

(c) Prompt no. (iii) asked. Replies, "No." Subject is asked," Is your drawing exactly right?" Replies, "I think so." Subject is asked, "Is there anything you have to guess at?" Replies, "No."

Comment. Measurement of lines but estimation of angles.

Robert   **Sub-stage IIIA**   **8 years 1 month**

1(a) Measures *AB* with ruler. Draws *AB* on own paper. Measures *DC* and *DB*. Marks *D* on *AB*. Measures *DC* again. Tries to carry ruler, holding angle constant, and draws in *DC*. Checks angle *BDC* by noting and marking point on ruler that *AB* cuts it, on the master copy, when the ruler is laid along *DC*. (See Fig. 10.) The ruler is then placed in a similar position on own drawing so that the corner is at *D* and *AB* cuts the same mark. Original estimated *DC* is erased and new one drawn along ruler placed as described, and shown in Fig. 10.

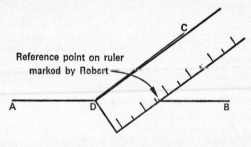

Reference point on ruler
marked by Robert

Fig. 10.

(b) Prompt question no. (iii) asked. Places ruler over each line in turn on master copy and own copy. Finally shakes head and says, "No, I think it's right." On checking by superimposition subject's copy is found to be precisely correct.

Comment. Necessity for measurement of angular separation realized and ingeniously carried out.

Alison   **Sub-stage IIIB**   **8 years 10 months**

1(a) Subject asks, "Do you want it to be the same size as that one?" This is
      confirmed. Child measures *AB* and draws it. Measures *AD*, sites *D*,
      measures *DC*, guessing size of angles, draws in *DC*.

 (b) Not applicable—child already using equipment for measuring.

 (c) Prompt question no. (v) asked. Replies, "Because the slope's wrong." Is
      now asked, "Can you think of any way of getting it right?" Tries the
      cardboard triangle provided but finds it of no use. Thinks; finally
      draws construction lines, as in Fig. 11.

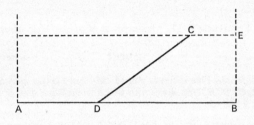

FIG. 11.

Then, having drawn *AB* accurately on own paper, child reproduced the
construction lines on her own paper, and having measured *BE*, *EC*,
and *AD* accurately, marked in points *D* and *C* on her own drawing and
drew *DC*. *DC* was then measured to ensure it was the correct length.

Comment. An interesting solution in which perpendiculars were correctly and efficiently used. Child placed at sub-stage IIIB because she did
not produce the solution on her first effort.

Martin   **Stage IV**   **9 years 10 months**

1(a) Measures *AB* with ruler and draws it. Measures *AD* and marks in *D*.
      Drops perpendicular *CK* on drawing no. 1, measures *BK* and *CK*.
      Transfers these measurements to own drawing and thus finds point *C*.
      Joins *DC*. (Fig. 12.)

 (b) Not applicable.

 (c) Prompt question no. (vii) asked. Child replies, "To find point *C*", and
      points to *C* on own drawing.

Comment. Use of the right-angle in measuring angle separation.

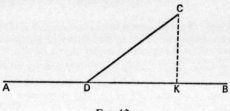

Fig. 12.

E. Experiment 5. The Measurement of Areas—Unit Iteration

Katherine   Stage I   5 years 10 months

Materials. Five different shapes cut from manilla card and marked *A, B, C, D, E.* Unit areas with which to measure. (See pp. 24 and 25, Figs. 5 and 6.)

1. Show shapes *A, B,* only. Say, "Which is bigger? This one [*A*] or that one [*B*]?" Point to them in turn. Record reply.
    Chooses *A* by pointing.
    Say, "Why do you think this one is bigger?" Record reply.
    "Because it's a square."

 (a) Say, "Can you tell any better using this [unit] card?" Record actions and comments.
     Looks at unit card and shapes *A* and *B*, replies, "No".
     Draw three or four squares inside *A* as an example for the subject if necessary.

 (b) Say, "You finish and find out how many squares there are in this one [*A*]."
     Record actions and comments.
     Cannot draw these squares despite assistance.

 (c) If subject cannot do this, complete the division of *A* into squares and help her to find out how "big" it is by counting up the squares.
     1(c) carried out by experimenter.

 (d) Say, "You use this square to find out how big this one [*B*] is." Record actions and comments.
     Cannot draw the squares; again drawn by the experimenter.

 (e) Say, "Would counting help you to find out if this one [*A*] was bigger than that one [*B*], or if they were the same size?" Record actions and comments.
     Says nothing—chooses *B* as the larger.

(f) Say, "If both were made of chocolate which would you choose?" Record reply.
Says nothing—chooses *A*.

2(a) Say, "Now find how large this one [*C*] is." Record actions and comments.
Experimenter draws in the squares and counts them with subject.

(b) Say, "What do you know about the size of these three [*A*, *B*, *C*]?" Record reply.
Points to *B* and says it is the biggest, *A* next, and *C* is the smallest.

3.   Remove *A*, *B*, *C*. Show *D* and *E* and the new units.

(a) Say, "Which is the larger, this one [*D*] or that one [*E*], or are they the same size?" Record reply.
"The same size."

(b) Say, "Now use any of these [unit] cards and try to measure the areas." Record actions and comments.
Is unable to use the units.

(c) If there is no attempt say, "Try the square card first." Record actions and comments.
Cannot use the unit indicated.

(d) Say, "Try the triangle or the other card." Record actions and comments.
Cannot use the unit indicated.
Comment. Unable to use the units. Child emotionally upset in 1(b) when she finds she cannot draw the squares. Did not recover from this disturbance throughout the experiment.

Edward   **Sub-stage IIA**   **7 years 10 months**

1.   Points to *B* at once. "Because it's longer."

(a) Places unit card in piece cut out of *B*, nods. "I still think this [*B*] is bigger."

(b) Draws in the remainder of the squares. On completion counts them, tapping each square with forefinger. "Nine."

(c) Not applicable.

(d) Starts at once to draw squares. On completion counts them.

(e) "This [*B*] is the biggest although the squares look the same size."

(f) "This one." [*B*]

2(a) Draws in the unit squares and counts them. "It's just the same size as these." [*A* and *B*.]

(b) "There's the same amount of squares in them." Subject asked, "Are they the same size then?" Replies, "*C* is the biggest, but *A* and *B* are the same size."

3(a) Places *E* on top of *D*. "They're the same size."

(b) Takes unit square and draws in squares in base of *E*. Takes triangle and after some difficulty draws in triangles in top of *E*. Does not divide *D* until experimenter suggests it. Is asked, "Which is the larger?" Replies "This one, *E*, because it has five squares in it, but this one, *D*, has only four." It is pointed out that not all the units in *E* are the same shape. Subject looks at them hard and states that *D* and *E* are both the same size.

   Comment. The units are used without transitivity. The child's performance is a good example of perceptual disparity outweighing numerical identity.

Anthony	Sub-stage IIB	8 years 7 months

1. "This one [*A*] because the other one has a piece missing."

(a) Tries fitting unit into irregular perimeter of *B*.

(b) Draws in remainder of squares and counts them aloud.

(c) Not applicable.

(d) Draws in the squares. Again counts them. "They're both the same."

(e) "They've got the same squares on them but they aren't the same shape. They are the same size."

(f) "Both because they're the same size."

2(a) Starts to draw in the squares at once. Completes them and counts. "They've all got the same number of squares."

(b) "They've all the same squares—they aren't the same shape. *B* looks the biggest but they're all the same size."

3(a) "The same size."

(b) Takes triangle and after a struggle fits it into the top half of *E*. Takes rectangle and fits it into the base of *E*.
Fits rectangle in *D* twice. States, "*E* is larger because its got more squares. than D" (i.e. equating rectangle and triangle units). Experimenter points out that neither of the units used is a square. Subject takes square and divides *D* into four squares. Examines *D* and *E*, "They're both the same size." (Four squares in *D* are equalled by one rectangle plus three triangles in *E*, i.e. 4 units equal 4 units although units are unequal in size.)

   Comment. Transitivity of units achieved but different sized units treated as equal.

Leslie   Sub-stage IIIA   **9 years 7 months**

1.   Looks carefully at shapes A and B—chooses B, "Because it's got bigger sides."

  (a)   "No."

  (b)   Completes drawing in the squares and counts them. "Nine squares."

  (c)   Not applicable.

  (d)   Draws in the squares carefully, counts them silently. Holds A and B one in each hand, "They're the same size."

  (f)   "This one." [A] "Why?" "Because bars of chocolate don't have an extra piece on." "Would you get any more chocolate by choosing A?" "No, you'd get the same amount."

2(a)   He draws in the squares at once and counts them.

  (b)   "They're all three the same size."

3(a)   "This is the largest." [E]

  (b)   Chooses triangular unit and divides the whole of E into triangles. Chooses square unit and divides the whole of D into squares. On completing this is rather nonplussed. Finally counts the seven triangles in E and four squares in D and states, "This [E] is the biggest." It is pointed out to him that he has used different units in D and E. "Oh, I ought to have used this [the triangular unit] in both." Divides D's squares into triangles and counts again. "This one's [D] the biggest, it's got one more."

    Comment. Transitivity and use of common measure, but unequal units are treated as equal until subject's attention is called to inequality.

Angela   Sub-stage IIIB   **8 years 6 months**

1.   Points to B—"That one, it's longer."

  (a)   Fits unit card into section cut away on B but does not appear to know how to use the unit. Is shown how to draw in squares.

  (b)   Completes drawing squares in A and asks, "May I go on and put squares in this one?" Proceeds to do so.

  (c)   Not applicable.

  (d)   Counts squares in both A and B without prompting, says, "They're both the same."

  (f)   "This one [A] because it's a square, but I wouldn't get any more chocolate—I might choose either."

2(a)   Takes unit square and places it, without marking, successively in position in C. Says, "It's the same as those [A and B]."

  (b)   "They've all nine squares, they're the same size."

3(a) "May I use these?" Points to unit cards. "I think this one is longer" points to D.

(b) Takes triangular unit and draws triangles on E, then turns to D and draws triangles on D. Counts up the triangles drawn in each shape, states, "That one [D] is the biggest because when you draw the triangles which are half squares, there are eight on that one [D] but only seven on that one [E]."

Comment. Operational unit iteration.

F. Experiment 6. The Subdivision of Areas and the Concept of Fractions

Brian   **Stage I**   **6 years 5 months**

Materials. A circular piece of plasticine (diameter 3 in. and about $\frac{1}{4}$ in. thick). Knife, matches, pieces of paper on which is drawn (1) a circle, (2) a square, (3) a rectangle.

1. Place the plasticine on the table.

(a) Say, "Let's pretend this is a cake. I want you to use these matches and divide [cut, share] the cake so that you and I will both have the same amount of cake to eat." (Show how to lay matches on plasticine if necessary but do not put in correct position.) Add, "How many pieces will you want?" if necessary. Record actions and comments.
   Divides cake into many small slices. When asked how many pieces are needed replies, "Two". Given a new cake but still persists in cutting into many small pieces.

(b) Say, "I want you to use this knife and cut the cake so that you and I will have the same amount of cake to eat." Add, "How many pieces will you want?" if necessary. Record actions and comments.
   After question subject replies that we want two pieces. Cuts cake into four unequal pieces, gives one piece to experimenter, takes one piece for self, pushes other pieces away saying, "We don't want that."

(c) Take the [two] pieces obtained from (b) and say, "Would all these bits taken together [illustrating by a sweep of the hand] make up as much as the whole cake?" Record reply.
   "No."

2(a) Say, "I want you to use these matches and divide [cut, share] the cake so that you, your teacher, and I all have the same amount of cake to eat." Add, "How many pieces will you want?" if necessary. "Are these all right?" If child realizes their inequality say, "Can you make them equal?" Record comments and actions.
   Divides the cake as per Fig. 13. It is pointed out that he has four pieces and not three. He cannot improve on this.

Fig. 13.

(b) Say, "I want you to use this knife and cut the cake so that you, your teacher, and I have the same amount of cake to eat." Add, "How many pieces will you want?" if necessary. Record actions and comments. Cuts as shown in Fig. 13.

(c) Say, "Would all these bits taken together [illustrate by sweep of hand] make up as much as the whole cake?" Record reply. "No."

3 Say, "Here is a drawing of a circle, a square, a rectangle." (Point out.)

(a) Say, "I want you to cut the circle into three equal parts [or pieces]. Draw lines where you think the cut should be, then cut it with the scissors." Record actions and comments. Cuts as per Fig. 14.

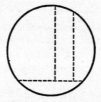

Fig. 14.

(b) Repeat 3(a) with square. Record actions and comments. Cuts as per Fig. 15.

Fig. 15.

(c) Repeat 3(a) with rectangle. Record actions and comments.
Cuts as per Fig. 16.

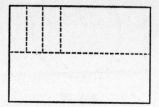

FIG. 16.

4(a) Say, "I want you to cut the circle into four equal parts [or pieces]. Mark the circle with your pencil and ruler and then cut it with the scissors." Record actions and comments.
Cuts as per Fig. 17.

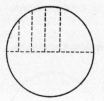

FIG. 17.

(b) Repeat 4(a) with square.
Cuts as per Fig. 18.

FIG. 18.

(c) Repeat 4(a) with rectangle.
Cuts as per Fig. 19.

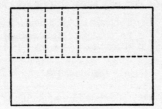

Fig. 19.

Comment. Problems of division into two equal parts. The subject was emotionally upset by his realized lack of ability to perform the operations required of him.

| Ian | Sub-stage IIA | 8 years 1 month |

1(a) Places matches correctly to divide cake into four. Is asked "How many pieces do we need?" Replies, "Oh!" Removes matches and replaces for bisection.

(b) Carries out dichotomy.

(c) "Yes."

2(a) "I shall need three pieces." Pauses to think. "I'll cut it into four." Places first and second match and accidentally places third match in such a way as to produce a fair trichotomy. Says, excitedly, "I've done it!"

(b) Cuts cake more or less accurately into three pieces.

(c) "Yes."

3(a) Marks centre of circle and bisects with pencil line. Realizes mistake and turns paper over. Thinks, says, "I can make four, but I can't make three." Thinks, states, "I can't remember how I did it last time, I can't do it."

(b) Traces with finger a double dichotomy. Marks middle of square with pencil. Bisects and starts to draw in diagonals. Realizes his mistake, announces, "I can make four pieces but not three."

(c) By trial and error using the ruler divides the rectangle into three equal strips across its length.

4(a) "Oh, that will be easy!" Performs double dichotomy at once.

(b) Performs accurate double dichotomy.

(c) Divides rectangle into four equal strips across its length.

> *Comments.* The problems of trichotomy well demonstrated. His immediate inability to remember his accidental discovery of the pattern used in 2(b) is interesting.

Irene   **Sub-stage IIB**   **9 years 1 month**

1(a) Performs dichotomy (slowly and thoughtfully).

(b) As 1(a).

(c) "Yes."

2(a) Divides cake into one half and two quarters. Disparity of sizes remarked upon by experimenter. Subject tries again. After continual rearrangement of the matches a reasonable trichotomy is effected.

(b) Effects trichotomy.

(c) "Yes."

3(a) Effects approximate trichotomy but one section is considerably larger than the other two.

(b) Marks off approximately one-third of the square then using a line at right angles to the first division, bisects the remainder. When asked to do so cannot think of an alternative method.

(c) Solution as for 3(b).

4(a), (b), and (c) Double dichotomy effected immediately.

> *Comment.* Trichotomy achieved by trial and error.

Colin   **Sub-stage IIIA**   **10 years 9 months**

1(a) Has some difficulty in understanding what is wanted—is looking for the "catch" as it seems too simple. "Oh, you want halves!" Effects dichotomy at once.

(b) Immediate dichotomy.

(c) "Yes."

2(a) Immediate trichotomy.

(b) As for 2(a).

(c) "Yes."

3(a) Immediate trichotomy.

(b) Attempts trichotomy by same pattern as in 3(a). Experimenter challenges the equality of the pieces. Subject immediately takes second square and divides into three equal strips.

(c) Divides into three equal strips across the length.

4(a) and (b) Double dichotomy carried out at once.

(c) Rectangle divided into four equal narrow strips across the width of the figure.

> *Comment.* Immediate trichotomy. "Perseveration" demonstrated in first attempt to answer 3(b).

APPENDIX 2

BOOKS AND ARTICLES BY JEAN PIAGET
(Translated into English)

(Arranged chronologically by the date of first publication in French.)

1924   *Judgment and Reasoning in the Child* (translated by Marjorie Warden), Routledge, reprinted 1951. (This translation first published 1928.)

1924   *The Language and Thought of the Child*, Preface by E. Claparède (translated by Marjorie Gabain), Routledge, 3rd edn. 1959.

1926   *The Child's Conception of the World* (translated by J. and A. Tomlinson), Routledge, reprinted 1951. (This translation first published 1929.)

1927   *The Child's Conception of Physical Causality* (translated by Marjorie Gabain), Kegan Paul, 1930.

1931   Retrospective and prospective analysis in child psychology (translated by E. W. Tait), *Brit. J. educ. Psychol.* **1**, 1931. (Discusses S. Isaacs, *Intellectual Growth in Young Children*.)

1932   *The Moral Judgment of the Child*, with the assistance of seven collaborators (translated by Marjorie Gabain), Kegan Paul, 1932 (new edn. 1968).

1932   Social evolution and the new education, *Educ. Tomorrow*, **4**, New Education Fellowship, 1932.

1936   *The Origins of Intelligence in Children* (translated by Margaret Cook), New York, International Universities Press, 1952.

1937   *The Child's Construction of Reality* (translated by Margaret Cook), Routledge, 1955.

1941   *The Child's Conception of Number* (translated by C. Gattegno and F. M. Hodgson), Routledge, 1952.

1945   *Play, Dreams and Imitation in Childhood* (translated by C. Gattegno and F. M. Hodgson), Heinemann, 1951.

1947   *The Psychology of Intelligence* (translated by M. Peircy and D. E. Berlyne), Routledge, 1950.

1948   *The Child's Conception of Geometry* (translated by E. A. Lunzer), Routledge, 1960.

1948   *The Child's Conception of Space* (translated by F. J. Langdon and J. L. Lunzer), Routledge, 1956.

1949   Psychological comments on the elementary teaching of natural science, *XIIth International Conference on Public Education: Introduction to natural science in primary schools*, Paris, UNESCO; and Geneva, IBE, 1949.

1951   The right to education in the modern world, *UNESCO: Freedom and Culture*, Wingate, 1951.

1953   *Logic and Psychology*, with an introduction on Piaget's logic by W. Mays, Manchester, University Press, 1953.

1953   Art education and child psychology, *Education and Art*, edited by Edwin Ziegfeld, Paris, UNESCO, 1953.

1955   *The Growth of Logical Thinking from Childhood to Adolescence: an essay on the construction of formal operational structures* (translated by A. Parsons and S. Milgram), Routledge, 1958.

1957   The significance of John Amos Comenius at the present time, *John Amos Comenius—Selections*, Paris, UNESCO, 1957.

1959   *The Early Growth of Logic in the Child; classification and seriation*, by Piaget and Inhelder (translated by E. A. Lunzer and D. Papert), Routledge, 1964.

1961   Children's thinking—the figural aspect and the operational aspect, *Natn. Froebel Fdn. Bull.* **127**, December 1960.

1961   The relation between perceptual and conceptual development, *Natn. Froebel Fdn. Bull.* **130**, June 1961.

1962   *Comments on Vygotsky's critical remarks concerning "The Language and Thought of the Child" and "Judgment and Reasoning in the Child"* Massachusetts, MIT Press, 1962.

Some Books and Articles about Jean Piaget and His Work

AEBLI, H., *The Development in Intelligence in the Child: summary of the works of Jean Piaget published between 1936 and 1948*, University of Minnesota Institute of Child Welfare, Minneapolis, 1950.

AEBLI, H., "Egocentrism" (Piaget) not a phase of mental development but a "substitute solution" for an insoluble task, *Paedag. Europ.* **3**, 1967.

ANON., A pattern of development in moral judgements made by adolescents derived from Piaget's scheme of its development in childhood, *Educ. Rev.* **19**, February 1967.

BEARD, R. M., Does Piaget count—in our number syllabus? *Teaching Arith.* **1**, Autumn 1963.

BEARD, R. M., The order of concept development studies in two fields, *Educ. Rev.* **15**, February/June 1963.

BEARD, R. M., The use of perception in mathematics teaching, *Maths. Teaching* **23**, Summer 1963.

BERLYNE, D. E., Recent developments in Piaget's work, *Brit. J. educ. Psychol.* **27**, February 1957.

BREARLEY, M. and HITCHFIELD, E., *A Teacher's Guide to Reading Piaget*, Routledge, 1966.

BRUNER, J. S., Inhelder and Piaget's "The growth of logical thinking". 1. A psychologist's viewpoint, *Brit. J. Psychol.* **50**, November 1959.

BURT, *Sir* C., Critical notice: The psychology of intelligence, by Jean Piaget, *Brit. J. educ. Psychol.* **31**, November 1951.

BURT, *Sir* C., Jean Piaget: pioneer of applied insight, *Times Educ. Suppl.* 2220, 6 December 1957.

CARPENTER, T. E., A pilot study for a quantitative investigation of Jean Piaget's original work on concept formation, *Educ. Rev.* **7**, February 1955. "A footnote" to the above article, by E. A. Lunzer, *Educ. Rev.* **8**, June 1956.

CHURCHILL, E. M., The number concepts of young children, *Researches and Studies*, **17** and **18**, January/July, 1958.

CHURCHILL, E. M., *Piaget's findings and the teacher*, reports of three conferences held at the Natn. Froebel Fdn. 1960, 1961. NFF 1962.

DIENES, Z. P., *Building up Mathematics*, Hutchinson, 1960. (Develops Piaget's views.)

DODWELL, P. C., The evolution of number concepts in the child, *Maths. Teaching*, **5**, November 1957. (Relevance of Piaget's findings to arithmetic teaching.)

DODWELL, P. C., The spatial concepts of the child, *Maths. Teaching*, **9**, April 1959. (Relevance of Piaget's findings to geometry teaching.)

DURKIN, D., Children's acceptance of reciprocity as a justice-principle, *Child. Dev.* **30**, 1959. (Discusses Piaget's *The Moral Judgment of the Child*.)

DURKIN, D., Children's concepts of justice: a comparison with the Piaget data, *Child. Dev.* **30**, 1959.

ELKIND, D., Quantity conceptions in junior and senior high school students, *Child. Dev.* **32**, 1961.

FLAVELL, J. H., *The Developmental Psychology of Jean Piaget*, with a foreword by Jean Piaget. The University Series in Psychology, Princeton, Van Nostrand, 1963.

GOODACRE, R. E. J. and E., What is reading readiness? (on Piaget) *Primary Educ.* **113** 3041, 16 February 1968; 3042, 23 February 1968; 3043, 1 March 1968.

HOLLOWAY, G. E. T., *An Introduction to 'The Child's Conception of Space'* (Routledge), NFF, 1967.

HOLLOWAY, G. E. T., *An Introduction to 'The Child's Conception of Geometry'*, Routledge, 1967, NFF, 1967.

HOOD, H. B., An experimental study of Piaget's theory of the development of number in children, *Brit. J. Psychol.* **53**, August, 1962. (Summary of thesis.)

ISAACS, N., *The Growth of Understanding in the Young Child: a Brief Introduction to Piaget's Work*, ESA, 1961.

ISAACS, N. *New Light on Children's Ideas of Number: the work of Professor Piaget*, ESA, 1960.

ISAACS, S., The Behaviour of Young Children. 1, With an appendix on children's "why" questions, by Nathan Isaacs (fifth impression), *Intellectual Growth in Young Children*. Routledge, 1948.

IVES, L. A., Meaningful learning; some notes on the Stern structural arithmetic apparatus, *Researches Studies*, **24**, October 1962. (Discusses Piaget's *The Child's Conception of Number*.)

KESSEN, W. and KUHLMAN, C., Thought in the young child: report of a conference on intellective development with particular attention to the work of Jean Piaget, *Monogr. Soc. Res. Child. Devel.*, 1962.

KING, W. H., The development of scientific concepts in children (No. 1 of a symposium, Studies of children's scientific concepts and interests), *Brit. J. educ. Psychol.* **31**, February 1960.

LOVELL, K., A follow-up study of Inhelder and Piaget's "The growth of logical thinking", *Brit. J. Psychol.* **52**, May 1961.

LOVELL, K., A follow-up study of some aspects of the work of Piaget and Inhelder on the child's conception of space, *Brit. J. educ. Psychol.* **29**, June 1959.

LOVELL, K., *The Growth of Basic Mathematical and Scientific Concepts in Children*, 2nd edn., University of London Press, 1962.

LOVELL, K., The philosophy of Jean Piaget, *New. Soc.* **8**, (202) 11 August 1966.

LOVELL, K. and OGILVIE, E., The growth of the concept of volume in junior school children, *J. Child Psychol. Psychiat.* **2**, September 1961.

LOVELL, K. and OGILVIE, E., A study of the conservation of substance in the junior school child, *Brit. J. educ. Psychol.* **30**, June 1960.

LOVELL, K. and OGILVIE, E., A study of the conservation of weight in the junior school child, *Brit. J. educ. Psychol.* **31**, June 1961.

LOVELL, K. and SLATER, A., The growth of the concept of time: a comparative study, *J. Child Psychol. Psychiat.* **1**, October 1960.

LOVELL, K. *et al.*, The growth of the concept of speed, a comparative study, *J. Child Psychol. Psychiat.* **3**, April/June 1962.

LUNZER, E. A., Recent studies in Britain based on the work of Jean Piaget, *N.F.E.R.* occasional Publ. 4, 1960.

LUNZER, E. A., Some impressions of Jean Piaget and his work, *Forum*, **4**, Summer 1962.

LUNZER, E. A., Some points of Piagetian theory in the light of experimental criticism, *J. Child Psychol. Psychiat.* **1**, October 1961.

MAIER, H. W., *Three Theories of Child Development:* the contributions of Erik H. Erikson, Jean Piaget, and Robert R. Sears, and their applications. *Harper International Student Reprint*, New York, Evanston and London, Harper and Row, Tokyo, Weatherhill, 1965.

MATTHEWS, G., We could do without exams (use of Piaget's *epreuves* in place of examinations), *Where*, **35**, January 1968.

MCLAUGHLIN, G. H., Psychologic, a possible alternative to Piaget's formulation, *Brit. J. educ. Psychol.* **33**, February 1963.

MCNAUGHTON, A. H., Piaget's theory and primary school social studies, *Educ. Rev.* **19**, November 1966.

NATIONAL FROEBEL, Experimental work on Piagetian lines, *Natn. Froebel Fdn. Bull.* **127**, December 1960. (Recent work in British and New Zealand schools.)

NATIONAL FROEBEL FOUNDATION, *Some Aspects of Piaget's Work*, NFF, 1955. (i) Children's ideas of number, summary by Evelyn Lawrence, Children's ideas of number, and The teacher and Piaget's work on number, by T. R. Theakston. (ii) The wider significance of Piaget's work, by Nathan Isaacs. (iii) Piaget and progressive education, by Nathan Isaacs. (Reprinted from the *Natn. Froebel Fdn. Bull.* **87–94**, April 1954–June 1955.)

PAGE, E. I. Haptic perception: a consideration of one of the investigations of Piaget and Inhelder, *Educ. Rev.* **11,** February 1959.

PEEL, E. A., Experimental examination of some of Piaget's schemata concerning children's perception and thinking, and a discussion of their educational significance, *Brit. J. educ. Psychol.* **29,** June 1959.

PETERS, R. S., Freud's theory of moral development in relation to that of Piaget. (No. 8 in a symposium on the development of moral values in children.) *Brit. J. educ. Psychol.* **30,** November 1960.

PHEMISTER, A., Providing for "number readiness" in the reception class, *Natn. Froebel. Fdn. Bull.* **135,** April 1962. (An experimental approach to teaching based on Piagetian investigations.)

RICHARDSON, E., Socialisation, aesthetic awareness and the development of literary appreciation, an application of Jean Piaget's theory of intelligence, *Researches Studies,* **20,** July 1959.

SIGEL, I. E. *et al.,* A training procedure for acquisition of Piaget's conservation of quantity: a pilot study and its replication, *Brit. J. educ. Psychol.* **36,** November 1966.

SIME, M., Architects of their own growth (experiment at Chorley College of Education using Piaget's methods), *Times Educ. Suppl.* 2657, 22 April 1966.

VAN ENGEN, H., The child's introduction to arithmetic reasoning, *Sch. Sci. Maths.* **55,** 484, May 1955.

VERNON, M. D., The development of perception in children, *Educ. Research,* **3,** November 1960.

VYGOTSKY, L. S., Thought and language, *Stud. Commun.,* Massachusetts, MIT Press, New York and London, Wiley, 1962.

WOLFF, P. H., The developmental psychologies of Jean Piaget and psychoanalysis, *Psychol. Issues,* vol. ii, no. 1, 1960, monogr. 5. New York, International Universities Press, 1960.

WOLINSKY, G. F., Piaget and the psychology of thought, some implications for teaching the retarded, *Am. J. ment. Defic.* **67,** September 1962.

WOODWARD, M., The behaviour of idiots interpreted by Piaget's theory of sensori-motor development, *Brit. J. educ. Psychol.* **29,** February 1959.

WOODWARD, M., Concepts of number of the mentally subnormal studied by Piaget's method, *J. Child Psychol. Psychiat.* **2,** December 1961.

REFERENCES

1. AEBLI, H., *The Development in Intelligence in the Child.* University of Minnesota Institute of Child Welfare, Minneapolis, 1950.
2. BURT, *Sir* C., Jean Piaget: pioneer of applied insight, *Times Educ. Suppl.* 2220, 6 December 1957. (Reproduced from *The Times Educational Supplement* by permission).
3. ISAACS, N., Piaget's work and progressive education, *Some Aspects of Piaget's Work*, NFF 1955.
4. ISAACS, S., The behaviour of young children, *Intellectual Growth in Young Children*, Routledge, 1930.
5. KNIGHT, R., *Intelligence and Intelligence Tests*, Methuen, 1950.
6. LOVELL, K. *Educational Psychology and Children*, University of London Press, 1960.
7. LOVELL, K. and OGILVIE, E., The growth of the concept of volume in junior school children, *Child. Psychol. Psychiat.* **2**, 1961.
8. LUNZER, E. A., Some points of Piagetian Theory in the light of experimental criticism, *Child. Psychol. Psychiat.* **1**, 1961.
9. PIAGET, J. *et al.*, *The Moral Judgment of the Child*, Kegan Paul, 1932.
10. PIAGET, J., *The Psychology of Intelligence*, Routledge, 1950.
11. PIAGET J. and INHELDER, B., *The Growth of Logical Thinking from Childhood to Adolescence*, Routledge, 1958.
12. THOMSON, R., *The Psychology of Thinking*, Pelican Books, 1959.
13. VERNON. P. E., *Intelligence and Attainment Tests,* University of London Press, 1960.
14. INHELDER, B., *Discussions in Child Development*, **1**, Tavistock Publs., 1953.